"Life's major accomplishments are made one ~~~~~ time. Thirty-one days is not long, but if you take daily steps you will make progress. Arlene Pellicane has walked the road and shares practical ideas on how to become a happy wife. I highly recommend this book to all wives who aspire for something better."

Gary Chapman, PhD,
author of *The Five Love Languages*

"This book captured my heart. Page after page holds real-life examples of ordinary women who discovered freedom, joy, and adventure through the challenging seasons of marriage. This book is filled with wisdom and inspires hope for wives and points us to the powerful and transformative love of Christ. Thank you, Arlene!"

Lynn Donovan,
speaker and author of *Winning Him Without Words*

"In this helpful and insightful new book, popular speaker and author Arlene Pellicane explains the awesome power of a happy wife. As with her other books, Arlene is positive, encouraging, specific—and talks about real life and real issues. Making the choice to become a happy wife will radically transform your world!"

David and **Lisa Frisbie**, executive directors
The Center for Marriage and Family Studies

"If you have ever longed for a better marriage, read this book. Arlene Pellicane masterfully unwraps five specific ways we can increase our happiness as wives. This book is filled with captivating examples, riveting interviews, biblical truth, practical action steps, and common sense advice. It's powerful to read alone, but even better when used as a group study with other wives who sincerely desire positive change."

Carol Kent,
speaker and author of *Becoming a Woman of Influence*

"Arlene Pellicane's message is every bit as clear, bright, cheerful, and wise as she is. Whether you're a newlywed or you've been married for ages, you'll find valuable, practical advice here. The daily format makes it easy to read, absorb, and apply the truths Arlene offers, and the examples from her own marriage and others' are honest, often funny, and genuinely helpful. Loved it!"

Liz Curtis Higgs,
best-selling author of *The Girl's Still Got It*

"Have you ever wanted to become a happy or even a happier wife? Maybe the key is for your husband to make some changes. Or maybe, just maybe, it has very little to do with him and a whole lot to do with you. If you're willing to apply the concepts presented in Arlene Pellicane's new book, you can become what you've wanted to become…a happy wife (and it may take only 31 days!)."

Kendra Smiley,
speaker, radio host, and author of *Live Free*

"Arlene relates to every wife in this inspiring, fun-to-read book that I couldn't put down. If you're ready to become a happy wife, and make the most of your marriage, she'll get you there in 31 days…guaranteed!"

Cindi McMenamin,
speaker and author of *When Women Walk Alone*

"Arlene empowers women with an important life-changing truth. You do have a choice not only on the actions you take but the attitudes you embrace. Many wives feel stuck in their marital unhappiness and can't find a way out. *31 Days to Becoming a Happy Wife* gives them a way out—practically, biblically, and winsomely."

Leslie Vernick,
counselor, speaker, and author of *The Emotionally Destructive Marriage*

"It's one thing to say 'I'm happy' and another thing to radiate happiness. I know Arlene and her husband, and they emit joy and epitomize the 'happily ever after' we all long for. *31 Days to Becoming a Happy Wife* really is an adventure, a path, a roadmap to a happy life! Arlene will help you find joy and satisfaction with practical, biblical advice and lots of ideas to make you smile."

Pam Farrel, author of 38 books,
including *Men Are Like Waffles—Women Are Like Spaghetti*

 to

Becoming a Happy Wife

Arlene Pellicane

HARVEST HOUSE PUBLISHERS
EUGENE, OREGON

Cover design by Left Coast Design, Portland, Oregon

Cover photo © Yuri Arcurs / Fotolia

31 DAYS TO BECOMING A HAPPY WIFE
Copyright © 2014 by Arlene Pellicane
Published by Harvest House Publishers
Eugene, Oregon 97402
www.harvesthousepublishers.com

Library of Congress Cataloging-in-Publication Data
 Pellicane, Arlene, 1971-
 31 days to becoming a happy wife / Arlene Pellicane.
  pages cm
 Includes bibliographical references.
 ISBN 978-0-7369-5806-6 (pbk.)
 ISBN 978-0-7369-5808-0 (eBook)
 1. Marriage—Religious aspects—Christianity. 2. Wives—Psychology. 3. Husbands—Conduct of life. 4. Happiness—Religious aspects—Christianity. 5. Wives—Religious life. I. Title. II. Title: Thirty-one days to becoming a happy wife.
 BV835.P455 2013
 248.8'435—dc23

2013023668

Printed in the United States of America

14 15 16 17 18 19 20 21 22 / BP-JH / 10 9 8 7 6 5 4 3 2

To Noelle and Lucy
May you grow up to be wives who truly live happily ever after.

Contents

Focus 5: Becoming Yielded

Do You Wish You Were Happier?

I'm not a natural on a bicycle. I have the distinct memory of riding my bike straight into a car when I was a girl. I'm thankful it was parked— I just didn't know how to turn! Years later, when I began dating James, I quickly learned how much he loved bike riding. He told me, "When I'm riding my bike and having the time of my life, I want to look over my shoulder and see you. I don't want to see my buddies. I want to see *you*."

That was enough for my little lovebird heart. I would become a cyclist. We went to the bicycle store to pick out a mountain bike for me. That was the fun part. But then I actually had to ride the thing. The first time I went on a trail, I had a hard time just transitioning from the parking lot to the trail. You had to steer between wooden posts, and I was terrified that I would run my bike right into one of the posts.

As I stared at those wooden posts in fear, they were getting closer and closer, and suddenly James yelled "Stop!" It was time for a coaching lesson. He told me five simple words that have served me well on the bike and in life.

You go where you focus.

He told me that if I was focused on the wooden posts, I would definitely steer myself right into them. But if I focused on the path between the wooden posts, I would safely steer my bike right onto the path.

You go where you focus. In life, if you focus on your problems, you will be filled with anxiety. But if you focus on what brings true happiness, you will be able to enjoy with newfound satisfaction this amazing journey of being a wife. It's time to focus on creating more happiness in your marriage.

Happiness Unpacked

What is happiness anyway? Is happiness a selfish or noble goal? Do you get it by being beautiful, wealthy, intelligent, or powerful? There are so many misconceptions about happiness. Just look at advertising, which lures us to buy products that promise a happy life. Yet happiness is not a product you can buy with a credit card. It's more like a by-product of how you live.

Let's compare what happiness is and what it isn't.

- Happiness is about contentment; it's not about comparison.

- Happiness looks out for others; it's not concerned only with itself.

- Happiness is at peace with God; it's not trying to win a popularity contest.

- Happiness is attained when you give it away; it's not achieved by hoarding.

- Happiness is saying thank you; it isn't saying I deserve better.

- Happiness can live in any circumstance; it doesn't have to have the exact right circumstances at all times.

- Happiness chooses to respect; it doesn't choose to retaliate.

- Happiness forgives; it doesn't warehouse grudges.

Being a happy wife has a lot more to do with belief than circumstances. That's good news! It means you can work from the inside out to produce more happiness and joy in your life. Maybe you're thinking, *You don't understand. I just wasn't born a happy person.* I do agree that some people are wired with sunnier dispositions than others. Some babies grow up to be Tiggers; others become Eeyores. But all you Eeyores out there take heart—even Eeyore can grow in joy from a "super-glum" day to a "ho-hum" day. Happy wives keep growing and learning, no matter what the starting place.

A.W. Tozer says, "The Christian owes it to the world to be supernaturally joyful." [1] That's certainly a spin on popular thought, which is better described as "The world owes it to me to make me happy." Many people view happiness as something they are *entitled to receive* instead of something they are *obligated to give*. When you believe in God, you have a direct connection to joy that can be given to others. Psalm 128:1 (HCSB) says this, "How happy is everyone who fears the LORD, who walks in His ways!"

It's Not Like Checking the Weather

My family lives in Southern California, and I must admit we're weather wimps. Oh, it's going to be 60 degrees today. Better wear long sleeves and a jacket. I'm constantly checking the weather to gauge what the kids should be wearing to school. Did you know we can "check the weather" when it comes to happiness in our marriage? You can measure your happiness as a wife by external events and circumstances, which, by the way, are many times out of your control.

> *Rainy weather:* Oh, I overslept and my husband didn't even talk to me before we parted ways this morning. Why is he like that? I am so unhappy!
>
> *Sunny weather:* My husband left me a note saying how much he loved me. He's going to take me out to dinner too. I have the best life!
>
> *Storm approaching:* We've been fighting for so long. How in the world are we going to work this out?

If you have to hold your finger in the air, checking the weather to determine whether or not you're going to be happy, you'll always be at the mercy of someone else. Here is a better way to take hold of happiness from Dale Carnegie's classic book, *How to Win Friends and Influence People*:

> Everybody in the world is seeking happiness—and there is one sure way to find it. That is by controlling your thoughts. Happiness doesn't depend on outward conditions. It depends on inner conditions. It isn't what you have or who you are or where you are or what you are doing that makes you happy or unhappy. It is what you think about. [2]

Happiness is not an external job. It's an internal one that has a lot to do with the way you think. This book is about changing your thinking and supercharging your faith. One word in this book's title is important to this process and it's not *happy*. It's the word *becoming*. Do you first believe that you are able to become a happier wife than you are right now? The word *becoming* has three different definitions that are very useful to consider:

Becoming means flattering. When you are a happy wife, you are beautiful and attractive.

Becoming means the process of coming to be something. You're not stuck. Get ready to spread your wings as a wife.

Becoming means proper, suitable, and fitting. It is fitting for a wife to act happy. It should not be strange or unusual.

The 5 Keys to Happiness for Wives

For the next 31 days, you're going to conduct your own happy wife experiment by focusing on five qualities represented by the acronym HAPPY. You are going to become more…

H = Hopeful

A = Adaptable

P = Positive

P = Purposeful

Y = Yielded

Hope acts as the foundation. You must know in your mind and heart that a happier marriage is within your reach and that your relationship with your husband can and will improve. Place your hope in God, not in your man or a plan, but in God.

Being *adaptable* is important because we wives aren't generally open to change and the twists and turns of life. But what if you could roll with the punches better? What if you could adapt easily and quickly to a variety of circumstances?

When you are *positive*, it's not only a fresh breath of air to your husband, it makes it easier to live with yourself. You know that being positive has many benefits, so it's time to learn more about optimism.

Purpose keeps you feeling alive. Maybe you've felt stuck in the same old, same old rut in your marriage. It's time to get a fresh vision of what you want to be as a wife and how to get there.

Lastly, a happy wife must be *yielded* to God and to her husband. When you allow God to take control of your heart and home, you experience the joy of being cared for by a loving heavenly Father.

How to Get the Most Out of This Book

You can read through this book in several ways. Please feel free to tailor your happy wife experiment with your schedule and preferences. You can read one chapter a day and complete the book in one month. Or perhaps you may want to read a few days at a time because you're on a roll. That's fine. Perhaps you can work through one letter at a time, such as reading Days 1–6 on becoming hopeful.

Read the affirmation for happy wives aloud once a day. You'll find this daily affirmation on page 189. Copy this affirmation and put it in different places to make it easy to recite daily. Tape it to your bathroom mirror, computer, or refrigerator. You will probably feel a little foolish the first time you read it out loud. But after a few times, it will sound more natural, and you will enjoy the benefit of putting positive thoughts about being a wife into your mind each day.

Start a Happy Wives Discussion Group. You can read the book together with a group of wives who also want to add more happiness to their lives. Use the discussion guide on pages 195-203. It's ideal to meet weekly for six weeks to discuss what you're learning and to have a good laugh together.

Do the action steps. New attitudes and actions go together. As you think differently about happiness, you are going to act differently too. At the end of each day's reading, you'll find brief sections called Today's Picture and Today's Prayer. As you think and pray about being a happier wife, you will see positive changes in your life that you're going to like.

Meditate on God's Word. I compiled a list of Bible verses about happiness and joy that you can read aloud and meditate on during the day. Turn to page 191 to see what the Bible says about happiness.

All right, dear friend, go ahead and give me a smile. That's fine—a great start! Get ready because in the next 31 days, you are going to find joy in unusual places and gain valuable insights about what really makes you happy.

My mom and I attend a weekly exercise spin class together, and believe me, there are many days when exercising and feeling happy don't go together. But our instructor always says, "Just get to my class and I will do the rest!" And it's actually true. If I simply get myself to her class, she will push me to exercise, and afterward I feel so much better.

So for this experiment in becoming a happier wife, allow me to give you that same encouragement. All you have to do is show up. Remember how I told you I wasn't a natural on a bicycle? You may not feel like a natural when it comes to happiness. Don't worry. All you have to do is focus on reading each day with an open and grateful heart. And let this book, working in concert with the Holy Spirit, show you how to be a happier wife one day at a time.

Are You a Happy Wife?

Before you begin your 31-day experiment in happiness, take a moment to assess how happy you are in your marriage today. Keep in mind there are no wrong or right answers. You don't have to impress or fool anyone, so be totally honest in your answers. Read each statement and mark if you mostly agree or disagree.

1. I believe that I have control over my happiness, not my circumstances.

   ☑ Agree   ❏ Disagree

2. My husband and I do not yell at each other or give each other the silent treatment.

   ❏ Agree   ☑ Disagree

3. I am flexible and can adapt easily to meet my husband's needs and to life's many changes.

   ☑ Agree   ❏ Disagree

4. I get enough rest each day and am in good health.

   ☑ Agree   ❏ Disagree

5. I am not jealous of other wives who may have more adoring husbands or more material possessions.

   ☑ Agree   ❏ Disagree

6. I enjoy making love to my husband, and being physically intimate really brings us together.

    ❏ Agree ☑ ❏ Disagree

7. I have not complained about my husband to anyone in the past month.

    ☑ Agree   ❏ Disagree

8. I think happiness is a skill I can learn and improve upon.

    ☑ Agree   ❏ Disagree

9. I have a clear vision of what I want in my marriage.

    ☑ Agree   ❏ Disagree

10. My family and friends would tell you that I smile a lot.

    ? ❏ Agree   ❏ Disagree

11. My husband and I go on regular date nights that are fun.

    ❏ Agree   ☑ Disagree

12. I believe my husband is the leader in our marriage.

    ☑ Agree   ❏ Disagree

13. I express prayers of thanks for my husband to God on most days.

    ❏ Agree   ☑ Disagree

14. After my husband has apologized sincerely, it's easy for me to forgive him.

    ☑ Agree   ❏ Disagree

15. If I run into an old friend, my face lights up as I describe to her what my husband is like.

    ❏ Agree   ☑ Disagree

Total the number of statements you agree with:

1-5: It's hard for you to remember when marriage was fun and easy. It seems like an uphill battle on many days, and you get tired of trying to make things work. Take this book seriously day by day with a sincere heart ready for change.

6-10: Things in your marriage aren't too bad, but they're not outstanding either. Your marriage is more stable than many of those around you, but you know it could be much happier. Make the decision that having an average marriage is not good enough for you. You want to take it to the next level and live with more joy at home.

11-15: You have a peaceful home and practice many habits of the happy wife. By making a few adjustments, you will radiate more joy and experience greater satisfaction in your marriage. Today life is good, and tomorrow will be even better.

Becoming HOPEFUL

A

P

P

Y

Day 1

Happiness Begins with Me

I waited patiently for the LORD;
he turned to me and heard my cry.

PSALM 40:1

There we were—my Realtor husband and me—standing in front of *our* new home, grinning and holding a bright red SOLD sign for the picture. The excitement of moving into a great house had temporarily eclipsed the massive stress of packing three weeks before Christmas. I couldn't see one thing wrong with my dream house.

And then we moved in.

The sink in the master bathroom started to leak. The plumber was supposed to come in the afternoon, but couldn't come until after dinnertime. While he tooled around under the sink, James and I were standing on top of our bed trying to fix the ceiling fan and light. My arms ached as I held up the light while James worked with the wiring. Let's just say it didn't work the first time (or the second, or the third). My dream home was ending up to be a lot of work.

Isn't that kind of like marriage? You marry Prince Charming and there's not a blemish on him. He looks perfect. And to be fair, there's not a blemish on you either, Princess. But as you begin to do life together day after day, you soon realize you need to put some elbow grease into the relationship to keep the magic alive.

Did working on my home diminish the joy of living at my new address? No, on the contrary, the work I put into my home makes me more satisfied and proud to call it mine. The fact that a marriage takes work isn't supposed to be negative. It's what makes it *real*. In fact, it makes it really good.

Mr. Wonderful

Do you remember when you realized you had met Mr. Wonderful? I fell in love with James in a pretty unusual place for twenty-year-olds— a nursing home. You might say he had me at Jell-O. One fateful Friday night, James and I were part of a van load of graduate students heading out to volunteer at the local nursing home. As he shared a story with the dozen or so elderly residents gathered in the recreation room, a few of them may have been dozing off, but I was fully awake. I prayed in my heart, *Lord, I really want to marry that man!*

We became good friends during those nursing home visits, Toastmasters meetings, and trips to Dairy Queen. But to my dismay, James told me in no uncertain terms that our relationship was totally platonic. It took me many months to release my feelings of love to God. After all, my stomach still did flips when I saw my "friend." But one day I told God, *I'm tired of hoping. I give up my dream of marrying James.*

A few weeks later, a funny thing happened. James asked me on a double date. Then he asked me on a real date. He was planning to tell me about his change of heart over an ice-cream blizzard at Dairy Queen, but thankfully an older and wiser friend lobbied for a better location. So over chocolate cake at Outback Steakhouse, he pulled out a yellow rose and a red rose from his jacket. He said he was glad we were friends and wanted to find out if there was *more*.

Less than a year later, we were walking down a center aisle saying those magic words, "I do." Boy, was I glad there was more.

Misplaced Hope for Happiness

James had a job in Dallas, so I moved from a dream job in Virginia Beach to join him. But I didn't mind, I was married! We lived in a one-bedroom apartment on the fourth floor, which we named the Love Nest. We were low on furniture but high on love. One day we even resorted to draping black garbage bags around our windows to simulate window coverings. They seemed to do the trick so we left them on for months. I was a happy wife even with black garbage bags around my windows and four flights of stairs to walk up and down each day.

My happiness wasn't dependent on fancy surroundings or a working elevator. I was just so happy to have someone to have and to hold forever.

Little things didn't bother me. Daily talks, kisses, and sweet nothings filled my love tank each day. But that natural happiness gradually diminished as bills and responsibility increased.

Can you relate?

Maybe instead of taking you out to dinner in the evening, your husband is staying late at the office again. He doesn't sit and give you his undivided attention like he used to. When he kisses you, sometimes you don't feel that spark. And if you're not careful, you might find yourself thinking, *You don't make me happy anymore.*

I love the story John Maxwell shares in his book *Make Today Count.* He and his wife, Margaret, had been married for a few years. He was speaking at a pastor's conference, and she was presenting a session for the spouses. He writes:

> During the Q and A time, a woman stood up and asked, "Does John make you happy?" I have to say, I was really looking forward to hearing Margaret's answer. I'm an attentive husband, and I love Margaret dearly. What kind of praise would she lavish on me?
>
> "Does John make me happy?" she considered. "No, he doesn't." I looked to see where the closest exit was. "The first two or three years we were married," she continued, "I thought it was John's job to make me happy. But he didn't. He wasn't mean to me or anything. He's a good husband. But nobody can make another person happy. That was my job." [1]

It's My Job

A happy you has to exist before there can be a happy wife. Happiness begins with a choice you make. When you wake up in the morning, you don't only decide what you are going to eat for breakfast. You decide whether you're going to be irritable or even-keeled, cheerful or melancholy. An attitude isn't thrust upon you. You have the great honor of choosing how you will respond in your marriage on any given day.

Author Cindi McMenamin said,

> When I wrote *When a Woman Inspires Her Husband*, I told my readers that for years I was praying that my husband would

change and adapt to me. I finally had to say, "God, change me. Make me the kind of wife he needs." When I became more adaptable, all of a sudden there was a different equation. Our marriage changed for good and I became a happy wife. [2]

Happiness in marriage can be found in some counterintuitive places. Through serving your spouse instead of waiting for him to serve you. Through seeking God instead of seeking your own good. Through making wise choices instead of waiting for great circumstances.

It's not up to your husband, your address, or your circumstances to make you happy. You are the one who ultimately makes the decision to choose joy. When you place your hope in your marriage to make you happy, you will be disappointed. But when you put your hope in God, you will find enough joy in Him to last you a lifetime.

A Clean Slate

It's easy to cave in under the pressure of the fixer-upper marriage and the less-than-perfect life. As you look around, you see a lot of people singing the blues about their marriages. Becoming a happy wife seems impossible on many days. Yet this desperation is where hope can really shine. Is it possible to regularly experience joy in your marriage? Can you really be happy in your current situation? If you are married to a decent man who is not abusive, I am here to tell you that happiness can indeed start with you. But you must begin by placing your hope in God.

Every New Year's Eve, more than one billion people around the world tune in to watch a ball drop about 140 feet down a flagpole. Why all the hubbub around a shimmering ball in Times Square? Perhaps it's because we are inexplicably drawn to the hope of new beginnings. A clean slate of 365 days, bright with no mistakes.

God is a God of new beginnings. Isaiah 43:18-19 says it so beautifully,

> "Forget the former things;
>   do not dwell on the past.
> See I am doing a new thing!
>   Now it springs up; do you not perceive it?
> I am making a way in the wilderness
>   and streams in the wasteland."

No matter where you are in your marriage, you can become a very happy, hope-filled wife. Now is the time for renaissance. I like how novelist Susan Meissner puts it, "Renaissance is a word with hope infused in every letter." [3]

Today's Picture

Remember the first time you kissed your husband? Let your mind dwell on that magical tingling you felt in the pit of your stomach. Picture yourself feeling this way again when you next see your husband today.

Today's Prayer

Lord, thank You for giving me a wonderful man in my husband. Help me to realize that it is not his job to make me happy. I give You my attitude and ask that You would help me choose joy every day and to take responsibility for myself. I do not want to follow the pattern of this world, but I want to be transformed by the renewing of my mind. Flood me with love for my husband today.

The Years Are Short

You have made my days a mere handbreadth;
the span of my years is as nothing before you.
Everyone is but a breath,
even those who seem secure.

PSALM 39:5

When was the last time you took your husband for granted? Chances are you didn't do that on purpose; it just happened. Sharon Jaynes reminds couples not to take each other for granted. Two years ago, her husband's father died. Six months later, his mother died. "We never know how long we're going to have with our spouses," Sharon says. [4]

Every day, every month, every year you have with your husband is precious. Just ask my friend Amy.

> My husband, Dan, had a joy for life, a joy for Jesus, and a passion for his work. If you met him, he was instantly your friend. He was authentic—that was the word we always used for people who were the same on the outside as they were on the inside.

Dan and Amy met through a mutual friend. They married in 1998 and became a blended family with serious girl power. Dan had four daughters and Amy had two. Dan called all the girls and Amy his "Magnificent Seven." In his early fifties, Dan enjoyed good health and exercised regularly, so when he collapsed in the living room watching Monday Night Football, no one could have guessed what would happen next.

A visit to urgent care and then to the hospital revealed the unthinkable: a tumor in Dan's head. Amy and Dan were praying for the best, but after the tumor was removed, one word sent them reeling. *Malignant.* The prognosis for someone in Dan's condition was from six months to three years to live. They chose to focus their thoughts on the Lord and His comfort and peace. Amy remembers,

> I wanted us to grow old together. I wanted us to share grandchildren, getting chubby and baking cookies and all that. I could very easily pound my fist and demand that God heal him. But I thought, you don't demand anything of God. I asked and left the results in His hands. But I remember thinking, *Lord, I don't know a finer man than the husband You gave me. If he completed his works here on earth, who am I to hold him from receiving his rewards in heaven?* Sure, you hope your life goes into your senior years—that's what you expect—but you could be called home at any time.

At one of their regular doctor appointments, Amy saw Dan's left arm go limp and her heart sank. The doctor told Dan that based on the symptoms, he had ninety more days. Yet even Dan's diagnosis could not dampen his indomitable spirit. He would say, "Who wouldn't envy my days? I get up and have breakfast and lunch and dinner with my best friend, Amy. I talk, walk, lift weights, read, and pray as long as I want."

Dan began to count his days, and once he went over that ninety days, he called them bonus days. He'd say, "I'm on number fifteen bonus day!" He'd not only keep track of his bonus days in his calendar, he would rate the days: A+ Day, Magic Day, Overjoy Day, and Golden Day. He used a point system to determine the rating, awarding points for such things as having a meal with Amy or hearing a bird sing in the morning. Amy recalls Dan asking her to sit on the patio to look around. He could see things she often never noticed.

Well Done

When Dan talked about heaven, he would say that Jesus was going to greet him with a cup of coffee and a pecan pie because those were two things his stomach wouldn't allow him to eat here on earth. Amy would joke back, "Remember, Jesus is a fisherman!"

Dan was doing well when he suddenly took a turn. Amy was forced to take him to a rehabilitation facility. Only two weeks later, she got a call.

The nurse said Dan's breathing was becoming laborious and she'd better come right away.

> I drove as fast as I could thinking, *Dan you'd better not die on me now without me being with you.* Even before the tumor, we had both said that we wanted the other person to give us our last drink of water and to be holding our hand before God ushered us home.
>
> I rushed into his room. He was unconscious and had an oxygen mask on, but he had this aura about him. He looked like he was being restored before my very eyes. I held his hand. I called his dad and his stepmom, and right after he heard their voices, he breathed his last breath and God took him home. I realized in that moment, Dan is seeing Jesus. And I hugged him and said, "Way to go, Dan. Good job."
>
> Dan wanted to hear more than anything in the world, "Well done, good and faithful servant." And I know he heard that and he was well. I knew he was experiencing such joy and I was so happy.

Did she say *happy*? How could Amy possibly rejoice in that moment of deep personal loss? She could see something that most of us miss. She understood that Dan was in eternity with Jesus and that someday she would also join him. That the good-bye is short and the hello is long.

> Dan was a gift to me. I didn't own him. The Bible says we are not our own, we were bought with a price. I got to borrow Dan and I know I'll see him again. Life is short, no matter how long you live, and before I know it, I'm going to see him again. [5]

Heaven and Earth

Psalm 39:5 tells us that a person's days are determined and "a mere handbreadth." A handbreadth is a measure of how wide your hand is—only about three inches. Look down at your hand. It's not very wide compared to the length of a football field or the Grand Canyon, is it? That's an imperfect example of how short your life on earth is compared to eternity. Somehow Amy knew that the pain she felt in losing her husband was short—a handbreadth—compared to the joy she would one day experience in eternity.

The next time you put lotion on your hands, pause for a moment. Consider that your life is a mere handbreadth. None of us own our husbands and can guarantee how long they will be with us on this earth. With the brevity of life in mind, are you making the most of each day as a wife? Don't take your husband for granted. Don't wait until tomorrow to make things right with him. Take a cue from Amy's moving story. Live your days as if they were Bonus Days or Golden Days or A+ Days.

The happy wife can have hope in all circumstances because she knows ultimately she's investing in a house not made with human hands. She's waiting to hear those words, *Well done, good and faithful servant.* If this is a difficult time in your marriage, hang on to hope and keep doing the right thing to build your husband up. Your good works will not go unnoticed by your heavenly Father. The sacrifices you make for the sake of your marriage today are small in light of the heavenly rewards in the future.

Today's Picture

Look at a photograph of your husband and imagine that his image is slowly fading away. How much will you miss him when he's gone? The day will come when your husband's time on earth is over. While he is here with you, make a decision to cherish him every day.

Today's Prayer

Lord, help me to number my days so that I might gain a heart of wisdom. I know I will stand before You one day. I want to live in such a way that when I go to heaven, I will hear You say, "Well done, good and faithful servant." Help me to cherish and appreciate my husband. I don't want to take him for granted. Thank You for giving him to me. Every good and perfect gift is from You, Lord, and I am so grateful.

Day 3

Tomorrow Starts Today

*You will surely eat
what your hands have worked for.
You will be happy,
and it will go well for you.*

Psalm 128:2 (hcsb)

When my daughter Lucy was three years old, she dreamt of the day she would go to Disneyland. We had shown her pictures of the famous theme park and told her we would be visiting Mickey and Minnie Mouse soon. Of course, she did not want to delay one second!

"Are we going today?" she asked with great excitement.

"No, we are going next week," I said.

Every morning that week, Lucy would wake up and immediately ask, "Is today tomorrow?" (Actually, it sounded more like "Is today tomowo?")

I laughed and told her, "No, today is not tomorrow yet."

The day finally arrived when we were leaving for Disneyland, and when Lucy asked her question, I replied with joy, "Yes! Today *is* tomorrow!"

In the same way my three-year-old Lucy wanted to experience the fun of tomorrow right now, we as wives sometimes dream wistfully of tomorrow.

Tomorrow we'll have more money.
Tomorrow he'll be more romantic.
Tomorrow we'll be happier together.
Tomorrow life will be easier.

Somehow we think something magical may happen to change our circumstance *tomorrow.* But in our heart of hearts, we know this is crazy thinking. Last time you heard, the fairy godmother wasn't making house calls on your street.

Have you ever thought to yourself, *I would be happy if…*? Sharon Jaynes says that's a dangerous lie many wives buy into.

> Think about Eve. She's the only woman who has had a perfect husband ever! And yet Satan came in the garden and said you will be happy *if*. I think that's what he does with husbands and wives. You will be happy *if* your husband is a different way. You will be happy *if* your husband does this for you. There are so many *ifs*! But you're not going to be happy until you're happy, and it has nothing to do with that husband. To be a happy wife cannot depend on your husband. It cannot depend on your circumstances. The only place you're going to find true happiness is with a relationship with Jesus Christ. When that happens and you let God be your source of happiness, you'll be a happy wife. [6]

Today Matters

If Eve teaches us what trouble happens when we say "I would be happy if…" maybe Abigail teaches us what good happens when we say "I am happy even though…" You see, Abigail was married to a very wealthy man—so far so good. But her rich sheepherder-landowner husband also happened to be cross, arrogant, dishonest, and wicked. The Bible tells us Abigail's story in 1 Samuel 25.

Abigail's name meant "my father rejoiced" while her husband Nabal's name meant "fool." Not exactly a match made in heaven. The Bible describes Abigail as beautiful and intelligent and Nabal as the antithesis. But something was about to happen to test Abigail. How she would respond on just one day would affect all her tomorrows thereafter. Allow me to set the scene.

Nabal was holding a grand feast for his sheepshearers. David and his men, while hiding out from Saul, had protected Nabal's shepherds from the Philistines in the wilderness. Hearing of the great bounty and thinking of his hungry men, David sent ten messengers to inquire if they could have food left over from the feast.

Nabal in his foolishness not only declined the request, he insulted the messengers. "Who is this David? Why should I take my bread and water and give it to men coming from who knows where?" Nabal roared.

David was enraged by this report and prepared four hundred men for battle to destroy Nabal's household. Meanwhile, one of Nabal's servants told Abigail all that had transpired. She acted quickly and sent her servants to intercept David with gifts of bread, wine, sheep, roasted grain, raisins, and figs to appease him. She herself took action—riding a donkey into a mountain ravine as David and his men descended upon her. She quickly dismounted and bowed down before David, apologizing for her husband's foolishness and acknowledging David's future kingship. Because of her wisdom and sound judgment, David accepted her apology. No blood was spilled. Abigail had saved her household.

Had I been married to Nabal, I might have thought, *Serves him right!* and I would have headed for the hills. But Abigail acted in hope to save her household, no matter how dysfunctional that household was. I think she understood that if she kept doing the right thing *today*, her *tomorrows* would work out. She didn't wait for someone else to do something. She didn't postpone or procrastinate on her plan. She took responsibility, not only for her own actions but for the foolish actions of her husband.

What you experience tomorrow has a lot to do with what you do today. Abigail wasn't waiting around, pining for her future to brighten. She acted with knowledge and wisdom each day. When you take responsibility for your own life, you possess hope for change. You're not a victim of someone else's shortcomings.

As for Abigail, she told Nabal all that had happened in her encounter with David. Nabal's heart failed him. About ten days later, God struck Nabal and he died. David then asked Abigail to be his wife. Notice how Abigail did not need to plot or plan to make these unusual events occur. She simply walked in wisdom each day, and God in His sovereignty secured this bright future for Abigail.

Don't Stop Believing

Maybe you're thinking, *I'm not as strong or brave as Abigail*, or *I don't have faith like her*. Perhaps her faith and resolve seem foreign to you. Don't let doubt get in the way of your happiness. Maybe you secretly think you don't deserve to be happy or that happiness is for other people. When you don't believe in a bright future for your marriage, you sabotage your marriage today.

When Jesus went to His hometown, the people couldn't believe He was a prophet. After all, wasn't He just the carpenter's son? It didn't make any sense that the son of Joseph and Mary could be divine. The Bible tells us He was amazed at their lack of faith and He could not do any miracles there, except lay His hands on a few sick people and heal them (Mark 6:5-6). Unbelief acts as a shackle, keeping you prisoner to anxiety and handicapping your joy. So the question is "Do you want to be set free?"

A man who had been an invalid for thirty-eight years lies near a pool called Bethesda in Jerusalem, along with many other disabled people who hope for a miracle cure (John 5:1-15). Jesus sees him and asks what seems to be a strange and obvious question, "Do you want to get well?" Was the sick man just going through the motions or did he really want to be cured?

Isn't it true that sometimes we don't want to be cured of our unhappiness? Our disappointments can feel comfortable. We're used to commiserating with friends. What would we talk about during coffee dates and dinner with the girls if we were, well, *happy*?

The chronically ill man told Jesus that he didn't have anyone to help him into the pool when the water was stirred. Jesus told him to get up, and immediately he was cured. Like that man, your tomorrows can be touched and changed in an instant by two words from Jesus: *Get up!* Have the faith to believe that God wants to bless your marriage and fill you with His joy. He wants to heal your brokenness and restore you to wholeness. But first you must want to be cured. You must be ready to act today in faith.

Zig Ziglar said, "If you don't see yourself as a winner, then you cannot perform as a winner."[7] Can you picture yourself as a winner, happy in your marriage? Do you want a bright tomorrow badly enough to make some positive changes today? Remember what my daughter Lucy asked, "Is today tomowo?" Yes, I suppose in a way it is. If you want to be happier tomorrow, you've got to start like a winner today.

Today's Picture

Take out two pieces of paper. On one sheet, write "I am an unhappy wife." On the other sheet, write "I am a happy wife." Now take the "I am an unhappy wife" paper and rip it up. You can stomp on those little pieces of paper if you want to! No longer will you hold on to this limiting belief. No longer will you believe the lie "I would be happy if…" You are a happy wife *today* because you can find something in your marriage to be grateful for now.

Today's Prayer

Lord, I admit sometimes I don't believe I can be happy in my circumstances. Forgive me for saying, "I would be happy in my marriage if…" Help me to be more like Abigail and do the right thing regardless of my husband's behavior. I believe You will work everything out for my good. Cure me of my unbelief and negativity. I believe You have the power to heal my emotions. I will be diligent to obey Your Word today, knowing that You will bless me in the future when I'm obedient.

Day 4

Facedown

Though you do not see Him now, but believe in Him,
you greatly rejoice with joy inexpressible and full of glory.
1 PETER 1:8 (NASB)

I was irritated by all the little things. I had to stand in a long line at the post office. Lucy had given me grief about taking her nap. I was cutting up chicken to put in a casserole for dinner. Why does it take so long to prep meals anyway? I was in a bad mood although I didn't really have a good reason for it. While I grumbled at the chicken, James was in the family room practicing his guitar. He was playing a worship song, and I began singing along.

My anxiety and irritation disappeared after just one verse. I was touched by singing that song about God's amazing love. The Holy Spirit filled my heart, and instantly I was at peace. All my striving could not produce happiness, but in a moment God filled me with that joy inexpressible and full of glory.

The Humility of Marriage

The Bible tells us in 1 Peter 5:5 that God opposes the proud but gives grace to the humble. Since marriage is an ideal place to humble yourself regularly, there are countless opportunities to receive God's grace! Author Poppy Smith remembers a time when she humbled herself before God in desperation. Born in England, Poppy grew up there and in Sri Lanka, Singapore, and Kenya. As a young woman, she was working in Nairobi when a handsome American walked into her church and her life. Poppy says,

> I think I was like many women. I was naïve and starry-eyed. You
> fall in love and you just want to get married and have babies. You
> don't really give much thought to compatibility issues because
> you assume you are.

Poppy was twenty-two when she married that dreamy American. Her husband, Jim, was thirty-two, and they quickly discovered they were about as incompatible as two people could be. He came from a conservative Christian home where women knew their place and kept house. Poppy grew up in a non-Christian home and had been a Christian only a few years. She was talkative. He was quiet. She had never been to the United States. He had never been to England. They moved to the US, and now Poppy was dealing with a new marriage, a new country, loneliness, regret, and anger.

Six months into their marriage, Poppy told Jim it was a huge mistake that they had gotten married. Even though they were committed Christians, they didn't know how to get along or how to meet each other's needs.

> I came to an emotional and spiritual crisis within my third or
> fourth year of marriage. I felt totally oppressed by my husband's
> expectations from his background. I was very lonely. He was
> gone constantly with his medical residency and he didn't know
> how to be empathetic with me. Within a couple of years I was
> pleading with God to show me a biblical way out of my mar-
> riage, but I couldn't find incompatibility as a reason. I thought I
> would have an emotional breakdown because I was so depressed
> or boiling angry. I just cried out to the Lord and He made it very
> clear: *Poppy, let Me change you. Instead of focusing on him and all
> the things you don't like about him, let Me work on you.*
>
> I had become someone I hated. I never expected to be an angry,
> bitter, resentful person. The things I would say were so cruel and
> demeaning. It took me being broken before God. I wanted to
> please the Lord, but I just didn't know how. [8]

Poppy had a deep desire to honor and obey Christ by loving her husband even though she was miserable in the marriage. When she humbled herself and said *Lord, change me*, she began to see her marriage turn around. That was forty-five years ago. Poppy laughs and says they've come this far because she stopped trying to change him. Instead, she asked God to show her what she needed to change. Many times God uses our present afflictions to make us humble. That humility can then make a way for hope and happiness.

The Tension of Ethan's Psalm

My firstborn is named Ethan and he was delighted to find Psalm 89, which was written by "Ethan the Ezrahite." The Ethan of the Bible begins his beautiful psalm by rehearsing the attributes of God and blessings of the believer.

> The heavens are yours, and yours also the earth;
> you founded the world and all that is in it.
> (Psalm 89:11)

> Blessed are those who have learned to acclaim you,
> who walk in the light of your presence, LORD.
> They rejoice in your name all day long;
> they celebrate your righteousness.
> (89:15-16)

But then Ethan laments that the king had been defeated in spite of God's promises:

> Indeed, you have turned back the edge of his sword
> and have not supported him in battle.
> (89:43)

> How long, LORD? Will you hide yourself forever?
> How long will your wrath burn like fire?
> (89:46)

Ethan's psalm depicts the age-old tension between the promises of a faithful God and the harsh realities of everyday life. Think of how this psalm applies to you as a wife. You know God has ordained your marriage and provided everything you need for its success, so why is it so hard to get along sometimes? Maybe you don't feel as if the Lord is supporting you in your marriage. You know intellectually that God reigns over everything, but why does He seem to be hiding from you? Why doesn't He intervene in your marriage?

Even with his questions and complaints, Ethan the Ezrahite ends his psalm with praise:

> Praise be to the LORD forever!
> Amen and Amen.
>
>   (89:52)

At the end of his venting, if you will, Ethan reasserts his praise to God. God is true and good. And as if one Amen (a proclamation of agreement or assent) weren't enough, he writes it again. *Amen and Amen.* Sometimes you must talk to your soul and encourage yourself in God's Word. When you choose to praise God, even when you feel abandoned or disappointed as a wife, God will bless you. When you're facedown in humility and desperation, He will lift you up.

Play It Loud, Sing It Loud

Sharon Jaynes recalls her first years as a married woman. When their son was little, her husband, Steve, would call her during the day just to say hi. Anxious to unload on someone, Sharon would pour out everything that had gone wrong in the day, even if it was only nine o'clock in the morning! After a while, Steve hesitated to call. He told her that when she told him every bad thing that had happened, it made him not want to call. Sharon says,

> I could have gotten mad about that. I could have stewed over it. But he was right. I can choose joy or I can choose to be miserable. Sometimes we need to have a good chat with ourselves. David talked to himself all the time in the psalms. He often starts out down, but then he reminds himself who God is and what God does. Put on praise music, read the psalms, and speak the truth out loud. Play it loud, sing it loud. It will put joy back in your life when you're feeling down in the dumps. [9]

Before you dump on your husband or stew in self-pity, you may want to have a good honest chat with yourself as the psalmist did. He asked himself,

Why, my soul, are you downcast?
  Why so disturbed within me?
Put your hope in God,
  for I will yet praise him,
  my Savior and my God.

(Psalm 42:5)

See how he continues to praise God even when he feels downcast and disturbed? If you humbly ask God for help and praise Him for His goodness, He will fill you with hope and lift you up. That's what I experienced that blah day when I was irritated while chopping up chicken in the kitchen. When you turn to God, He turns everything around.

Today's Picture

Picture your home in a children's storybook and envision the sky filled with phrases between your house and heaven. Those sentences are lifting right up to God and they are words of praise. Imagine that your home is a place of praise to God. Whenever God looks down upon your home, He is pleased with that sweet aroma of praise heavenward.

Today's Prayer

Lord, I praise You that the heavens are Yours and the earth also is Yours. You founded the world and all it contains. My home is Yours. I dedicate it to You. I praise You for the husband You have given me. I humble myself before You and ask for You to be glorified in my home. I love You and thank You for watching my home closely with Your tender care.

Turn It Off

Whatever is true, whatever is noble, whatever
is right, whatever is pure...
think about such things.

PHILIPPIANS 4:8

When James and I were first married, he had an unusual request. Could we spend the first three months without a television? The request seemed outrageous. Not only did I love watching television, I worked producing feature stories for a national television show. However, James convinced me that life and work would continue on track even without episodes of *ER*. I soon discovered something very important early in our marriage. I didn't miss the television. In fact, I thoroughly enjoyed the peaceful environment of our home.

It's been fifteen years since we made that agreement, and we *still* don't watch television in our home. We do have a TV and a DVD player, but we've never subscribed to cable. Sure we've missed out on a lot of popular culture and entertainment. We don't know who *The Bachelor* picked, why the *Desperate Housewives* were so desperate, or what's happened in *The Office*. We're basically *Lost*. But we do know what is happening in each other's lives in high definition. Plus we've skipped a lot of the negativity that enters a home through popular shows. Not many producers in Hollywood have your marriage's best interests at heart.

Technology has charged ahead of us—inventing new convenient ways to watch your favorite programs and movies on multiple devices. You can spend hours on social media sites, such as Facebook and Pinterest, connecting with "friends" while your flesh-and-blood husband sits alone in the other room watching sports.

Consider this relational equation:

More screen time = Less marital satisfaction
Less screen time = More marital satisfaction

Now before you get too defensive, I'm not saying you should throw your smartphone, computer, or TV out the window. But I am asking, *Would your life improve if you unplugged more often?* If much of your free time is spent in front of a television, computer, tablet, or mobile device, how does that impact the quality of your marriage? Maybe the television is a constant companion chatting away in the background. Your computer is an oasis so you don't have to interact face-to-face with anyone, including your spouse. Keep in mind social media may be very antisocial for your marriage. You may not realize it, but screen time may be robbing you of the time and tenderness that you desperately long for.

Stealing Time

Each of us is given twenty-four hours a day. No more, no less. Whether you have an extraordinary marriage or a mediocre one, you get the same amount of time as everyone else to invest in that marriage. According to a Nielsen report, the average American spends more than thirty-four hours a week watching live television, plus another three to six hours watching taped programs. That's as much as forty hours a week of television! [10]

Think of all that time that could be spent in more meaningful ways. What if you watch only fifteen hours of television a week? You could still take half those hours and use that time to take a walk around the block with your husband, go on a dinner date, or snuggle up on the couch together with great books.

Zig Ziglar described television as the "income suppressant." [11] James calls it the "stupidvision." In the right amounts, television can be a welcome diversion and a way to laugh or be touched by something profound. But at the average rate of thirty-four hours a week, let's call it what it is: a waste of time.

Relationship Killers

For my book *31 Days to a Happy Husband*, I interviewed actor Kevin

Sorbo (*Hercules: The Legendary Journeys, Soul Surfer*). He said this about television's portrayal of the family man:

> Hollywood does such a great job of demasculinizing men. If you look at any sitcom, that guy's an idiot. He's a moron. His kids are all rolling their eyes. They've done that for decades. Kids grow up watching that and they think fathers are idiots. You look before with *Father Knows Best* or *My Three Sons*, the dad had smart things to say to his kids. He was a moral man who led by good example. For some reason, it's become funny to make the dad fat and stupid. [12]

When we watch sitcoms that ridicule many of the values we believe in, our relationships suffer. Slowly we believe the story lines we watch on our favorite shows. *Fathers are inept. Women are smart and deserve more. Sex should be enjoyed often and with whomever you find attractive.* Are these the stories you want to fill your mind with?

Hours of screen time, day after day, with the television or computer will undoubtedly cause your relationship with your husband to weaken. It's easy to escape and envision a better life. If only your home looked like the photo on Pinterest. If only your husband were as handsome as the lead actor. Counselor and author Leslie Vernick says it's important for a woman to be aware of the stories she is telling herself. Here are four common stories, according to Leslie:

> *Story line 1: I should be better than I am.* That's a huge story that women tell themselves. I should be a better mother. I should be a better wife. I should be thinner, smarter, a better housekeeper. Whatever it is, I should be better than I am, so I'm constantly unhappy because I can never be enough.

> *Story line 2: Life should be better than this.* Things should be better than they are. If we're constantly in that mindset, we're going to be disappointed. We're not handling now. Because now should be better than it is. We're not looking for the positive and the things we can grow from. We're just constantly negative because it should be better than this.

> *Story line 3: Life should be easy and fair.* People don't want to have to work at things. Hollywood does not want to teach us that marriage is hard work. They want to teach us that it's all romance. If

you have passion and a great sex life, that's all it takes. That's just not true. Life isn't easy and it's not fair.

Story line 4: I deserve more than I have. We live in a very strong entitlement culture, so we constantly think we deserve more. I deserve a better husband. I deserve a better house, more money, more happiness, more whatever! Then we can never be grateful for what we have. What we have isn't enough. We deserve more. [13]

When you tell yourself any of these stories, which are constantly reinforced by television and movies, you become more and more unhappy with your life. One way you can begin rewriting your life story is by turning off the negativity, lust, greed, and self-centeredness you find rampant on television and in movies today.

The Curfew

Though James and I don't get cable, we can easily spend an hour or two wasting time online in the evenings. We realized that after we put the kids to bed at night, we were retreating to our computers. Individually in separate rooms, we answered emails, browsed Amazon, checked Facebook, and watched YouTube videos.

One night James said, "I'm on the computer all day, why am I wasting time at night on this thing?" He proposed—as you can perhaps guess—a solution. We would try a computer curfew. At a reasonable time, such as thirty minutes after the kids went to bed, we would turn off our computers. Neither of us is particularly productive at night. My ability to write has pretty much expired after nine o'clock.

Sometimes we miss the computer curfew, but we follow it most evenings. Turning off the computer earlier in the evening is rejuvenating. It feels good to swap screen time for rest. Sometimes we lie in bed together reading books. Other nights, we give each other massages. And of course, we have more time for intimacy, which certainly counts as quality time.

So the next time you're aimlessly flipping through channels or clicking through social sites online, stop yourself and ask a few questions:

- What could be a better use of my time right now?

- Does this activity help or harm my relationship with my husband?

- Would anybody really care if I didn't watch this program or didn't show up online?

When you turn off your electronic devices more often, you'll turn on other things in your marriage such as creativity, quality time, compassion, and stronger connection. Think on what's true, noble, right, and pure. If you dwell on those things and not the nightly news or a crime drama, you'll be a hope-filled, happier wife.

Today's Picture

You and your husband are sitting in the living room. You are not watching television or using your phones. Neither of you is online with the computer or a tablet. Your husband has his arm around you, and you are talking to each other and kissing occasionally. This is what ten minutes of free time can look like. Try it for yourself later on today!

Today's Prayer

Lord, I quiet myself in Your presence. I am still and I know You, God. Forgive me for being more attached to my cell phone and social networks than I am to Your holy Word. I want to have fewer distractions in my life. Show me when I'm wasting time. Show me how I can spend more quality time with my husband. I will think about what is true, noble, right, pure, lovely, and admirable in my marriage today.

Day 6

Envy Slayers

Resentment kills a fool,
and envy slays the simple.

Job 5:2

When Cindi McMenamin and her husband attended their first marriage conference, Hugh realized something about his wife. She responded to words of affirmation and physical touch. Ready to put something he learned into practice, he printed the words "Talk more, touch more" on a piece of paper and taped it on his car dashboard as a reminder. Cindi saw it one day and asked, "What's this?" You can imagine her delight when her husband explained it reminded him of what she needed every evening when he got home. [14]

Hugh happens to be a pastor so you might chalk up his sensitivity to being a minister. You might think, *My husband doesn't do anything like that.* Without warning, your mind can be tempted by envy, which Aristotle defined as "pain at the good fortune of others." [15]

Robber of Happiness

When your friend tells you about her Mediterranean cruise with hubby, does your heart sink or swim? Are you able to genuinely rejoice with someone or do you quietly long that you could swap experiences? None of us would say to a happily married friend, "I hope your marriage goes south." Yet if trouble came to her door, perhaps secretly you would find a little comfort. *Good, her life isn't perfect either.* Envy can blur our vision, causing us to long for something we don't have and to desire that others not have it either. Envy robs us of happiness. Proverbs 14:30 says it this way,

> A heart at peace gives life to the body,
> but envy rots the bones.

Maybe you're a Christian but your husband is not. Or your husband isn't the spiritual leader you'd like him to be. You fight the urge to envy wives who have a spiritually strong husband and God-centered marriage. Lynn Donovan, coauthor of *Winning Him Without Words: 10 Keys to Thriving in Your Spiritually Mismatched Marriage,* knows what that is like.

Growing up in a Christian home, Lynn had a relationship with church but not with God. In her twenties, her faith wilted. She met and married an unbeliever who was vastly different from her, and for the first few years, they were very happy. They were living for their careers and vacations. But eventually Lynn became restless. The world was proving shallow, and God was wooing her home.

> I ran home to the faith of my childhood and dragged along behind me my unbelieving husband who was kicking and screaming all the way. To say he was miffed about the "new man" in my life is an understatement. Around the time our daughter was born, conflict about church, faith, raising our daughter, and all kinds of things stepped up because my values were now being sifted by the Bible. I realized when you live with your best friend and the love of your life, but you have at the core different values, that's extraordinarily challenging. How do you negotiate that?

Going to church by herself was hard for Lynn. Surrounded by couples and families, she felt like the oddball and it just about wrecked her. But she turned to God, asking Him to take away her pain and bring her husband to faith. She's been married more than twenty-one years, and her husband's seat at church is still empty.

> There were days when I said I cannot do this one more day. It is a slow process, and I think God does that on purpose because He wants to make sure we get the lesson and it sticks. For me it was reading God's Word and catching the lies I believed that my husband should be this perfect man. He should always make me happy. As I put the truth inside and let go of some of the lies, that's when the joy began to come. I wasn't living to be fulfilled by my marriage anymore. Often women come into marriage

and think, *Here's my Prince Charming. He's going to fulfill all of my dreams.* Now I was asking God to do that. There's joy when you let God come into your life even when things are rough in your marriage.

Lynn's husband has come so far, even enthusiastically supporting her work as a Christian author writing about being in an unequally yoked marriage. He gave her his full support to help couples with different faith perspectives get along as they have learned to do. Instead of envying other Christian marriages, Lynn has chosen to rejoice in her own.

> The longer I have walked this unequally yoked journey, the more I have watched the Word of God be proved true. In the early years, I tried to use my words. That did not go over well. That just created more conflict. You know what works? Love. Through my transformation of just loving my husband, he could see I wasn't trying to manipulate him and he could finally relax. I didn't feel it was my responsibility to save him, and he felt freedom because he didn't feel like he was a disappointment to me. We had peace in our marriage. The hostility went away. And now my husband is free to discover Christ on his own. I can't wait to get up and see what God's going to do today. It's a blast![16]

I hope you can hear the joy in Lynn's voice. She isn't wasting her life, pining away for a God-fearing man. She doesn't sabotage the Christian marriages around her because she's bitter about being in an unequally yoked marriage. She presses deeply into God's Word and counts on His faithfulness. Envy cannot grow in that environment of faith and joy.

Envy's Opposite

I have always thought of contentment as the opposite of envy. When you are happy with what you have, you are not envious of others. You're content with your portion in life. But to take it one step further, perhaps the opposite of envy is saying to others, "I'm so happy that you have been so fortunate!" It's rejoicing with those who rejoice.

Do you have an abundance or scarcity mentality when it comes to happiness? Do you think there's only so much joy to go around, and if your neighbor has the lion's share of happiness in her marriage, somehow your shot at happiness is diminished? Friend, God specializes in multiplication. When you rejoice with others about their relationships and successes, God multiplies joy in your life.

True Christian love banishes envy from our hearts. When the apostle Paul defined love in 1 Corinthians 13, he included this description: "[Love] does not envy" (1 Corinthians 13:4). However, without the love of Christ, it's all too easy to slip into envy. As Paul says elsewhere,

> At one time we too were foolish, disobedient, deceived and enslaved by all kinds of passions and pleasures. We lived in malice and *envy*, being hated and hating one another. But when the kindness and love of God our Savior appeared, he saved us, not because of righteous things we had done, but because of his mercy (Titus 3:3-5).

Because of what Christ has done, you can have tremendous hope. Hope for eternal life. Hope in the here and now. Stop believing the lie that joy is only for someone else. It's for you too.

Today's Picture

Is there a wife you envy? Maybe you wish you had a close marriage like she does or that you didn't have to work. Bless that woman in your mind and heart. Picture yourself hugging her and rejoicing in the good things God has given her. Remember, there is not a shortage on happiness. God uses multiplication. The more you rejoice with others, the more reasons you will have to rejoice yourself.

Today's Prayer

I surrender my feelings of envy to You, Lord. I'm sorry if I have compared myself unfavorably to other women. I am not only content with what You've given me, I choose to rejoice with those who rejoice. I know that joy is for me. I accept Your gift of joy and thank You for filling my heart with hope for the future. You are waiting to show me mercy, and You rise to show me compassion. I believe You want to bless me and my marriage.

Focus 2

HOPEFUL

Becoming ADAPTABLE

P

P

Y

I'm Not Budging

They made their hearts as hard as flint and would not listen...

ZECHARIAH 7:12

B efore getting married, my idea of camping was sitting in a casual cafe overlooking a lake before returning to a rustic motel. James's camping experience was vastly different. He remembers carrying his tent and food in his backpack and finding a different spot under the stars every night. Yikes!

As you can imagine, our first camping trip had its share of tears, conflict, and compromise. We were newlyweds living in Dallas. The young couples group at church was going on a camping trip. While we drove toward the campsite, I was sullen, quiet, and irritable. It was painfully obvious that this camping trip was not my idea. We had packed the tent (which James had put on our wedding registry), but I had left my smile back at our cozy apartment.

James pulled the car over right before we entered the campground. He turned off the engine and looked at me sternly. "Are you going to act like this all weekend long? Because if you are, we can just turn around and go home."

I mumbled through tears, "You mean I didn't have to come?"

I still laugh today when I think of that moment. I collected myself and realized I was being selfish. I promised to have a better attitude. When all the camping-loving wives greeted me, I hugged them back and smiled weakly. Although the weekend didn't make me a camper, I survived and made some funny memories with my outdoorsy husband.

I was discovering that in a happy, two-way-street marriage, you have to be willing to budge. Being able to adapt to your spouse (and vice versa) is a valuable skill it pays to learn.

Adjustments and Modifications

The words *adjustments* and *modifications* may sound like they come from a manual for robots or a build-it-yourself computer. But all of us must admit, as human beings, we could use some occasional tweaking and minor changes. We must learn to adapt to our ever-changing circumstances and also to the needs of our husbands.

When you're single, you can get along doing things your way. But when you are united with someone in marriage, the Bible says the two shall become one flesh (Genesis 2:24). That translates into some serious adjustments and modifications! In a marriage that works, you must constantly adapt to the needs of each other.

One day I was working out at home to a fitness DVD. The instructor on the DVD said you have to force your body to adapt. You have to force it to make changes. When you're doing jumping jacks and your body tells you to stop, your mind has to tell your body what you want it to do. That's a great picture of marriage. Sometimes you want to throw in the towel or say something that you shouldn't, but you must force yourself to adapt. You must adjust. Life isn't just about you anymore. "You" have become a "we." And to be a happy "me" in the "we," you must learn to adapt according to what's best for your marriage, not just for yourself.

Remember Lynn Donovan in the spiritually mismatched marriage? She wanted her daughter to attend a Christian school. But her husband felt strongly that she should go to public school. Lynn prayed about it and adapted to her husband's wishes. Their daughter is eighteen now and loves Jesus with all her heart. Lynn trusted the Lord, adapted to her spouse out of respect, and is reaping benefits in her close-knit family.

It's also helpful to adapt what we expect from our husbands. Leslie Vernick has a happy marriage, but it hasn't always been a happy soul-mate kind of relationship.

> I know his strengths and I know his weaknesses. They used to really bug me early in our marriage. I would complain and criticize and all that. He didn't change them and it only made our marriage worse. So I've accepted that he's not a handyman. He's

not going to help me in the yard; he hates gardening. He's going to watch more TV than I would choose to watch.

But these aren't deal breakers. This is part of learning the attitude of forbearance. In any good relationship, you forbear with one another's weaknesses or differences. We have accepted who each other is and we're not trying to change each other. That's a tremendously freeing thing. My husband isn't trying to make me into his ideal wife, and I'm not trying to make him into my ideal husband. [1]

Put Your Will into Drive

When I asked Liz Curtis Higgs if she'd ever said in her marriage, "I'm not budging!" both of us had a good laugh. Liz replied,

I'm afraid there have been lots of times when I've put my foot down and said I think it should be done this way. But I've discovered that when I do that, Bill loves me enough to say, "Okay, we'll do it your way." And then after a bit, I realize this was not a good idea to begin with. I am learning there are hills worth dying on, but most of them are not. I guess that's what twenty-seven years of marriage does. You find out the stuff that really matters. When you say, "I will not be moved on this," there's got to be a biblical reason why. It can't just be because I want this.

Liz travels extensively, speaking to thousands of women every year. Since she travels so much, she doesn't need a car. Liz says Bill is extraordinarily frugal, so having one car for the two of them worked out great. But one day, Liz headed out to her driveway to go somewhere when she realized Bill had the car. She was stuck.

When Bill got home, Liz said, "Maybe we need to think about getting a second car." He said that was fine but that the car needed to be inexpensive since it wouldn't be used that much. Liz realized she had to lay down her dream of having a nifty car to zip around town. She asked the Lord to find them a car that would make both her *and* Bill happy. And now Liz is the proud owner of a ten-year-old car with tons of miles on it, but at least it's a red Mini Cooper! Liz says,

I could have been a real pill and found ten reasons why I needed a new car, but that would have been stupid. We don't need a car payment. We don't need a new car in the driveway. This one is perfect. Sometimes it's a matter of compromise—a happy medium, if you like those words better. How can I get what I want and still make this wonderful man of mine happy?[2]

Sometimes you have put your will into drive. Naturally you may want that new car (or whatever it is you are wanting right now). But the wise woman can adapt to achieve what's best for her family.

In Zechariah 7:8-10, we read that God wanted the people to show mercy and compassion to one another. He did not want them to oppress the widow or the fatherless. He did not want them to plot evil against each other. But the people refused to listen. They did not adapt and they made their hearts as hard as flint.

Flint is a hard gray rock that in ancient times was used for tools or weapons. As wives, our hearts over time can harden like flint. We can say things like *I will not budge. I will not cooperate. I will not adapt.* That unwillingness to change can become a weapon of war in a marriage. Don't let that hardness ever form around your heart. Be willing to change and open up your life to endless possibilities.

Today's Picture

When it comes to being willing to work with your spouse, are you hard like flint or soft like clay? Which object describes you better?

Today's Prayer

Lord, make me an instrument of love in my marriage. Help my heart to be soft like clay, willing to adapt to Your will in my life. Mold me into something beautiful for You. Help me to be adaptable. I don't want to be stuck in my ways. I want to grow. In Jesus's name, amen.

Day 8

Satisfaction (Not) Guaranteed

I have learned the secret of being content in any and every situation.
PHILIPPIANS 4:12

I love shopping at Costco. Not only do I get to munch on samples, if I don't like something I can return it, no questions asked. My satisfaction is guaranteed! Have you noticed that marriage isn't like that? Your satisfaction is *not* guaranteed. You can't stand in line to return your spouse or exchange an irksome quality for a better one. Some days in marriage, you feel like the luckiest woman alive. On other days you wonder, *Did I really think that burping thing was funny when we were dating?*

The other morning we were getting the kids ready for school. Ethan is in third grade and Noelle is in first, and we live close enough to our school that we can ride bikes there. James came over to the sink and started doing the dishes. I said, "Oh, I can do the dishes. You get the bikes out."

"I wouldn't want you to get an allergic reaction to doing dishes," he said.

You know when your husband says something that rubs you in every wrong way possible? How dare he say that to me!

"I do dishes every day!" I said.

"Oh, you do?" he replied as he walked to the garage.

The kids thought this was very funny. When Ethan rode off to school on his bike, he yelled back at me, "Good-bye, allergic reaction!"

While James was gone with the kids, I was fuming. Granted, I'm no stellar housekeeper. Not even close. The only thing I actually do with consistency is dishes. So that's why I was so upset by what he said. I felt as though he was making fun of my ability to keep the house clean and that he attacked my only success: an empty sink.

I had a good talk with myself, and when James walked through the door, I calmly said, "I was really hurt by your comment. I have an allergic reaction to lots of things around the house, but doing the dishes isn't one of them. That's like me telling you that you have an allergic reaction to meeting with your real-estate clients."

He understood and apologized. Like most husbands, he didn't mean to stir up so much emotion by his glib comment. When you live with a person day after day, you're bound to say something flippant that you didn't really mean. The key is to apologize and begin with a clean slate again and again. Satisfaction in marriage isn't guaranteed, but it can be achieved with some elbow grease and grace.

This Isn't What I Signed Up For

When her children were young, Pam Farrel's husband, Bill, worked as a youth pastor at a large church. Life was good. Then Bill felt called to be a senior pastor, so in his twenties, he became the senior pastor of a church of fifty. It was an exciting opportunity for him, but it meant major changes for their young family. They left the three-bedroom house Bill had remodeled and made beautiful and moved into a small apartment with strict rules in a metro area. Children were not allowed in the backyard, patio, front yard, or grass areas. It was as if children were not allowed to exist. Bill had the car, so Pam was home with two rowdy boys, ages two and four, without wheels to escape. Pam says,

> Normally I'm optimistic, but depression just blindsided me. One day I went into the walk-in closet, and I couldn't remember what I went in there for. I sat down on a pile of dirty laundry, and then my two little boys came in. Brock asked, "Mommy, what's wrong?" I told my four-year-old that I didn't know. I just wrapped my arms around those two little guys and sat there crying until they fell asleep.
>
> I said, *God, this is ridiculous.* I have two healthy children. I have a husband who loves me. And it's amazing he still loves me because when he comes home, he hears things like, "Why did you bring me here? Why do we have to live like this?" *God, You have to give me an answer to my pain.*

Pam went to the kitchen table with her Bible. She prayed, *God, give me a fresh glimpse of who You are.* She decided that day to keep a journal and write down every place in the Psalms where she saw God's love for her. That gave her inspiration to look for verses elsewhere in the Bible about how she could show love to Bill. She read in Ephesians 5:33, "the wife must respect her husband." Pam wondered,

> Is there a loophole for something like this? I took out all my Bible study tools, because I was looking for the loophole. Instead of finding ways to opt out of "the wife must respect her husband," God told me, "Pam, I want you to see Bill as I see him: as a man worthy of honor. I want you to speak to Bill as I would speak to Bill: words of encouragement to build him up. I want you to serve Bill: help him succeed at this new calling."

After this clear encounter with God, Pam called Bill and asked him to meet for lunch. She explained what God had been telling her and told him that from this point on, she was 100 percent committed to be on his team.

> I told Bill, "Honey, if I don't get the stuff, if I don't get the house, if I don't get the car, it's okay." Bill did the happy dance! After that talk, he went into high gear. He found a way to move us from an apartment to a condo with a yard. He then bought a property and hammered up a two-story, three-bedroom house by himself while pastoring. I think all of that was easier since he wasn't hearing me complain day after day after day. It was like jet fuel to his heart. It changed him. More than anything, it changed our relationship because we were both easy to be around. We both were highly productive. [3]

Are you in need of some jet fuel for your heart? I suggest following Pam's example. When you feel dissatisfied in your marriage, don't complain, nag, kick, or scream. Seek God and try to see your husband through the eyes of Christ.

Adaptable Paul

The apostle Paul had plenty of reasons to be dissatisfied in life. He became a missionary so that people could hear the good news of Christ. He experienced imprisonment, beatings, hunger, sickness, and great need. The believers in Philippi had lapsed in their financial support of Paul. When they followed through in their commitment to giving, Paul doesn't question them. He's gracious.

> I rejoiced greatly in the Lord that at last you renewed your concern for me. Indeed, you were concerned, but you had no opportunity to show it (Philippians 4:10).

He gives them the benefit of the doubt. Imagine if your husband forgot your birthday, and you gave him an out by saying sincerely, "Oh, I'm sure you wanted to get me something, but you just didn't have the opportunity."

Paul continues,

> I am not saying this because I am in need, for I have learned to be content whatever the circumstances. I know what it is to be in need, and I know what it is to have plenty. I have learned the secret of being content in any and every situation, whether well fed or hungry, whether living in plenty or in want. I can do all this through him who gives me strength (Philippians 4:11-13).

Matthew Henry in his commentary on this passage writes, "This is a special act of grace, to accommodate ourselves to every condition of life, and carry an equal temper of mind through all the varieties of our state." [4] In God's strength, you can learn to adapt to the disappointments and dissatisfactions experienced in marriage. Fixing your eyes on Christ as your example, you will be able to experience real, long-lasting satisfaction in your marriage—even when your husband says you have an allergic reaction to dishes.

Today's Picture

Think of the areas in your marriage in which you are highly satisfied. Maybe your husband is a great cook, kisser, provider, or listener. Make a list of five things you appreciate about your man:

1.

2.

3.

4.

5.

Today's Prayer

Lord, my husband isn't perfect and I'm not either. There are times when we are going to disappoint each other. Help us get through those times and unify us as a couple. Thank You for my husband's many strengths. Show me what my husband looks like through the eyes of Christ. I choose to be content in any and every situation. I can do all this through Christ who strengthens me.

Rags, Riches, and Everything In Between

*I delight greatly in the L*ORD;
my soul rejoices in my God.
For he has clothed me with garments of salvation
and arrayed me in a robe of his righteousness.

ISAIAH 61:10

One year for James's birthday party, he wrote on the invitation, "Don't bring gifts, just cash!" You should have seen the small bills and coins that came in response. But the creativity award went to our friends who brought a small, potted topiary with bills hanging from the leaves. We had our very own money tree. If only it worked.

Money can be a source of joy or anxiety to a couple, a marriage builder or destroyer. There are financial seasons of plenty and seasons of want. You have to be able to weather both in order to be a happy wife. Some years, you fly to a resort and enjoy a weeklong vacation. Other years, you might pitch a tent in the backyard and eat s'mores by moonlight. The key is being able to savor it all.

The Industrious Wife

If the wife described in Proverbs 31 were alive today, she might be featured on the cover of a business magazine. She works long hours, selects her own raw materials, buys properties, invests her assets, and gives to charity. Getting up early, she makes food for her family and servants. She works vigorously throughout the day, sells linen garments, and does not eat the bread of idleness. There is obviously much to learn from this virtuous and industrious model of a wife. For now, let's zero in on one verse that can help us experience happiness in rags or riches.

> She considers a field and buys it;
>> out of her earnings she plants a vineyard.
>>>> (Proverbs 31:16)

Notice that she *considers*. She doesn't rush into the next get-rich-quick scheme. When I was in graduate school before I married James, I sat in a sales presentation for gumball machines. By the end of the presentation, I envisioned myself putting gumball machines in several locations, making hundreds of dollars a month selling candy while I slept. It seemed so easy. Buy the gumball machines, fill them with candy, collect the money, refill the candy, and repeat. I spent a small fortune on my gumball machine empire that day.

It didn't take long for me to figure out that placing my money-making-gumball-machines in strategic locations was next to impossible. Franchises had strict rules and profitable spots were already taken. Months later, after contacting dozens of businesses, I had been able to place only one gumball machine in my hairdresser's salon. Once a month, I collected my candy profit, which usually amounted to a few dollars. I ended up donating all the gumball machines to local youth groups. My first start-up had failed miserably. (James does not allow me to attend sales presentations by myself anymore.)

I hadn't done my homework like the Proverbs 31 wife. I saw the gumball machines as a magic bullet instead of a business. She *considered* her field before she bought it. She didn't buy anything until she had figured out if it was worth her money and whether she could afford it. If we as wives simply asked, *Is this worth my money?* and *Can I afford this?*, it would probably save us a nice chunk of change.

Using her earnings, the Proverbs 31 woman planted a vineyard. She didn't run into debt to plant her vineyard expansion. She didn't blow her extra money; she used it to reinvest. The happy wife adapts her spending as paychecks increase and decrease. She fights against debt and lives within her means with an eye to saving and investing for the future.

Financial Foreign Languages

Maybe you've tried to have money conversations about spending and saving with your husband, but your money talks turn into money fights. You feel as if you're speaking different languages. Well, according to financial advisor Bethany Palmer, you probably are. In their book *The 5 Money Personalities*, Bethany and her husband, Scott, outline five money personalities: saver, spender, risk taker, security seeker, and flyer. By understanding your and your spouse's money personality, you can save yourself tears and strife.

Bethany shares the example of when Scott went to purchase a $150 Blu-ray player. At the store, Scott learned an $800 cable went along with that nifty player. Being a saver and security seeker, he was sweating bullets about that large unexpected purchase. But he came home with that cable followed by the Geek Squad to install it.

When Bethany heard the story, it didn't faze her. She's a spender and a risk taker. She was thinking, *Let's just do it*. But when she saw how uncomfortable Scott was with this unplanned expense, she wisely said,

> Let's just tell the Geek Squad this isn't a good time. We'll figure out if there's a better way. I was speaking Scott's money language (saver, security seeker), not mine. If we spoke my language, the Geek Squad would have stayed because I was satisfied. But if you want a happy relationship, you have to learn to speak the other person's money language also.

> Money impacts about every decision we make, from big things like that cable to boring things like cups of coffee. You can't go any day without making money decisions. Couples don't divorce over 401(k)s; they get divorced because of the nitpicking and nagging, when we can't understand how we handle money in day-to-day decisions.

Bethany has seen many women dig in their heels about money decisions, unwilling to change or accept fault. She recalls a conversation she overheard between two women at a salon.

> One wife was complaining, "I sent him to the store and I just wanted lightbulbs. He came back with shoelaces, milk, tennis balls, and a candy bar. I just asked him to get the stupid lightbulbs!" I wanted to say to her, "Your husband is a spender. If you don't like that, don't send him to the grocery store to get lightbulbs. Maybe you need to say lightly, 'Oh, honey, you're a

spender. Next time I'll go to the store and get just the lightbulbs.'"
Isn't it better to learn to understand each other? [5]

Do you and your husband fight often about money? Perhaps it would benefit you to talk about your money personalities in a nonthreatening way. There's no right answer or right combination of money personalities. The victory comes in understanding each other and working as a team to achieve your financial goals.

Rich Rewards

The Bible has a lot to say about money. Of the thirty-eight parables of Jesus, at least a dozen are devoted to money and to our use of material goods. Approximately one of every eight verses in the Gospels deals with the subject. [6] In Proverbs 31, we read that this wife doesn't bankrupt her family with overspending. On the contrary, she makes her family more prosperous. "She watches over the affairs of her household and does not eat the bread of idleness" (Proverbs 31:27). As a result of her abilities and initiative, her husband and children praise her. She is honored and praised at the city gate.

The book of Proverbs opens with "The fear of the LORD is the beginning of knowledge" (Proverbs 1:7) and ends with "A woman who fears the LORD is to be praised" (Proverbs 31:30). Here's the secret to the overall success of the Proverbs 31 wife. It's not business school experience, a large inheritance, or a millionaire husband. The secret is the fear of the Lord. The happy wife doesn't put her trust in her husband or her finances. She places her trust in God while learning how to be financially productive. And she's even more valuable than a money tree!

Today's Picture

Imagine yourself holding a $100 bill. You hear someone's voice describing you as financially responsible, a hard worker, and a wise investor. You are good with money. You can be trusted with wealth. Next time you hold money or a credit card, remember these thoughts. You will not squander your earnings nor make money more powerful than it should be in your life.

Today's Prayer

Lord, Your Word says a lot about money. I don't want to love money or make it a god in my life. Help my husband and me to work together to use our money wisely. Give us this day our daily bread. I place my trust in You and ask You to bless us financially with everything we need.

Day 10

No Miss America Here

This young woman, who was also known as Esther,
had a lovely figure and was beautiful.

ESTHER 2:7

When my daughter Noelle was three years old, we were vacationing in Virginia Beach. While in a clothing store, Noelle looked at herself head to toe in the mirror, smiled approvingly, and exclaimed, "Beach Babe!" I didn't even know she knew that phrase. Right on cue the saleslady brought me a T-shirt that said "Beach Babe" across the front. Although I was glad Noelle was happy with her appearance, I did not buy the shirt.

As we get older, we usually lose that enthusiasm over our body image that Noelle displayed that day. We wouldn't dare wear a T-shirt that said "Beach Babe!" Who can live up to that? The definition of beauty from popular culture leads us to believe *I fear I am NOT wonderfully made* instead of *I AM fearfully and wonderfully made*. If we allow them, our physical shortcomings can sabotage our ability to be happy in our own skin.

In the Bible, we read about the beautiful Esther, who became the new queen because the king was attracted to her above all others. She had to complete twelve months of beauty treatments before meeting the king. No wonder she became the "Miss America" of the kingdom. We're lucky if we get fifteen minutes to put on makeup.

Celebrity Chef?

Not only can we fall short in the beauty department, we might not have the domestic abilities of the perfect wife either. I remember once when James came home from grocery shopping after work. On the shopping list, I had written *rotisserie chicken*. I figured we could throw something together with the chicken for dinner. When James got home, he was in his kitchen sergeant mode, boiling water for pasta and telling the kids to start cutting vegetables and washing fruit. As he was preparing the meal, he asked bluntly, "What were you planning to make for dinner?"

"Rotisserie chicken," I muttered.

"And what else?"

"I don't know."

I could tell he was irritated that I did not have a plan for dinner.

The next day, he gave me a pep talk about how I needed to think about these things and plan a menu. He then asked me, "What would a celebrity chef do?"

"A celebrity chef would order someone to make their food," I said flippantly.

"No," he said. "You've got to think like a celebrity chef. They plan what's going to be eaten and they are prepared."

I'm steaming now. *I'm supposed to be like a celebrity chef? I don't think so!*

He told me to imagine if I were out speaking all day and he had been home with the kids. If I came home and all that was served for dinner was rotisserie chicken, wouldn't I be disappointed?

Now I'm starting to feel a wee bit convicted because I know I could do a better job with meal preparation. I told him I would try harder with meal planning and also shared that it would have helped me if he could have brought it up in a different way. Maybe something like, "Hey, sweetheart, I've noticed meal times have been tough to pull together. It would be great if we could eat more vegetables and maybe add another side dish like pasta. Is that something we could do in the future? How can I help with that?"

He said that was fair. It's so easy to think of all your spouse's shortcomings (he's so demanding) when confronted with your own (I'm a lousy cook). As James said that night after he told me he wanted better meals, "There's no good time for a man to tell anything to a woman."

Liz Curtis Higgs remembers her first Sunday with Bill as a married couple. They had come home from church, and Bill threw himself on the couch, grabbed the paper, and said, "What's for dinner?" She laughed and said, "Wow, whatever it is you're going to fix!"

Cleaning House

Liz describes herself as a lame housekeeper (I can certainly relate to that!) and offers some helpful tips about cleaning house:

> I got my family to help with the household stuff. I made it pretty clear from day one with the kids, this is not a hotel where you're waited on and clean laundry just appears. This is a home. We always had lists on the fridge, and everyone jumped in.
>
> Every other Thursday, I welcomed through our doors two amazing women who cleaned the nooks and crannies. I know some people say that's great if you can afford it. I did this before I could afford it. I decided it mattered more to me than a manicure or a lunch out. It mattered more to me than a lot of things. If hiring outside help is not feasible, team up with a girlfriend and help each other. Every other Tuesday it's her house, then it's your house. It gets done and you're having fun.
>
> Let go of perfectionism. Because the sad story is that after the house is clean, I walk around and smell the clean air and enjoy the clean surfaces, but I know full well in forty-eight hours, it's going to look like my house again. That's okay because people live here. It's not a showplace; it's a home. [7]

You and your husband may have different standards when it comes to keeping house. Carol Kent's husband is neat and orderly. Gene is his name and hygiene is his nickname! Here's how Carol found meaning in cleaning:

> Gene grew up in a home where they were always remodeling. His dad always had unfinished projects. There would be dust everywhere, flannel blankets instead of doors. He was embarrassed to have friends over. He lived in a state of chaos. The home was untidy and there were piles of things everywhere.
>
> I realized one of the things that brings my husband joy is when our home is cared for, everything is neat, the sink is empty, and the beds are made. That gives him a sense of joy and a kind of security. It makes me happy to keep him happy by keeping the house looking good. I also recognize that he is very quick to be a partner. This is a team effort. [8]

Package Deal

One way to make your household run smoother is to identify what roles you and your husband are good at. Marjorie Blanchard encourages wives to consider how they are wired and what they enjoy doing in the home.

> I know a lot of folks who fall into some pretty traditional roles, like the man being in charge of finances and the woman being in charge of the social life. In some cases, it might be better the other way around. My husband is much better at socializing. He loves to plan trips. I am better at organizing things. I am better with money. It's a matter of finding out what you are good at and bringing that into the marriage.
>
> Leadership is an inside-out job. The more you understand yourself and the more you understand the kind of person you are, the more you're able to talk about it with your spouse. [9]

Maybe it's time for you and your spouse to let go of unrealistic expectations of what the "perfect" wife is like. Liz Curtis Higgs says it's about appreciating what you do have and not whining about what you don't have.

> Our husbands are imperfect, just as we are. We have to give them the grace that we extend to ourselves. When Bill and I make each other a little crazy, our standard line is "Package Deal." If you've got all these qualities that you love in your spouse, then you've got to deal with the other ones and say it's part of the package! [10]

Accept the package you are as a wife. Rejoice in the way you are designed. Play to your strengths. Adapt your expectations to reflect what God is asking you to do and to become in your marriage, not what popular culture dictates. You are one tremendous package deal!

Today's Picture

Imagine a stress-free home where you and your husband share the tasks of cleaning, cooking, maintaining your home, budgeting, and planning the calendar. In this mental utopia, which tasks are suited for you and which tasks are better suited for him?

Today's Prayer

Lord, You know my weaknesses when it comes to keeping house. Help me not to resent certain duties in my home. Give me wisdom to recognize what I should delegate and what I should do on my own. Forgive me for sometimes complaining and feeling sorry for myself. Help me to simplify my home life and to prioritize what is truly important to my husband and me. Give us grace to work together as a team.

Sex Yes, Dishes No

Take me away with you—let us hurry!

SONG OF SONGS 1:4

It's late in the evening. You're standing by your kitchen sink, starting to rinse off the dishes. Your husband walks in the room and gives you that look. He says something like, "Let's go in the bedroom. I'll take care of the dishes tomorrow." What's your first reaction? Are you thrilled for the opportunity to ditch the dishes for your sex life? Or would you rather keep at the task at hand and save sex for another time?

I have to admit I like getting my tasks done and checking off my to-do list. So I tend to stay at the sink with the dishes and sometimes miss opportunities to be more romantic with my husband. One person I can learn from is Pam Farrel, coauthor of *Red-Hot Monogamy*. Pam says,

> The first step is to realize that red-hot monogamy is a gift that God gives to a husband *and* a wife. It's not a duty. It's not like the dishes. It's not like the laundry. It actually is something God made to bless you. When you get that in your mind, it's easier to want red-hot monogamy because you realize God wants to bless you. Your husband wants to bless you. This is a good thing. Give yourself permission to be that sexual woman who enjoys sex because it's a gift from God.
>
> I think sometimes women get stalled in that they don't think they could or should enjoy sex. God could have wired us so that our anatomy worked only for reproduction, but He wired our bodies so that sex would be enjoyable. I think that shows God's love

for us. When the relationship with your husband is the highest relational priority on your plate, it puts everything else in proper perspective. [11]

What if you want sex to be an important part of your marriage, but you still feel unfulfilled? When I interviewed sexual therapist and author Joyce Penner for my book *31 Days to a Happy Husband*, she gave this advice to wives:

> One of the games we women play is to think, *If he really loved me, he'd do this and do that*, rather than taking responsibility for ourselves and understanding when is it that we've had the best times sexually? What makes it the best? What can I do to make sure that happens? How can I prepare for that?
>
> Many women have false expectations about themselves and their husbands, whether it's from having read romance novels, watching movies, or having previous sexual experience before marriage. They are looking for what we call dopamine-driven sex, the adrenaline sex that just zaps you and overtakes you. If you don't feel those kinds of feelings, you think, *He just doesn't turn me on*, and you shut down. Married sex doesn't function on that romance-novel type of response. It functions on a much deeper, connected intimacy. [12]

We can escape to a steamy, unreal fantasy life in the world of novels. It's soft porn for women and it is poison in a marriage when your husband doesn't measure up to the man in your fantasies. You've got to shake yourself free of any influence that threatens the sacredness of the marriage bed.

Got Your Salad Kit?

Kathi Lipp, author of *The Husband Project*, has a great idea to keep the spice in your love life. She and her husband, Roger, bought different lotions and oils with flavors like guava peach and lemon. Roger said that it sounded more like stuff you would put on a salad. From then on, they called it "the salad kit." So when they're traveling, they can say "Did you pack the salad kit?" without being embarrassed in front of the kids. Every couple needs a good salad kit!

Another pantry item is a little more embarrassing. Here's Kathi talking about what one mother of a preschooler shared about her intimate apparel:

> I asked the audience how you can make your husband happier. We were on the topic of lingerie, and one woman said, "I have a tip on when you want to save money on your edible underwear." You could have knocked me over with a feather. Wow, that's never been a concern of mine. What budget envelope does Dave Ramsay assign to edible underwear? Is it food? Entertainment? Clothing? I don't know. So I'll give you the tip. She buys fruit roll-ups and cuts them out herself and makes her own underwear. [13]

So there you have it. An unexpected use for fruit roll-ups! Creativity along with a sense of humor can go a long way in the bedroom. Women love to create anything from table centerpieces to photo collages, floral arrangements to fanciful cupcakes. Why not use that God-given creativity in your sex life? The more you invest in creating intimate moments between you and your spouse, the happier you'll be behind closed doors.

Seize the Moments

I've heard that it's difficult to have a great sex life when your kids are young, but I'm thinking it's got to be even harder when they are teenagers. Now my kids are three, six, and eight, and they go to bed early. They have no idea what we are doing when we shut our door at night. So mothers of preschoolers, now is the time to attack your husband. Do not delay and miss this opportunity, because when the kids are teenagers, they'll still be awake long after you retire for the evening. They'll be aware of every sound in the house. I've heard from parents of teenagers that you have to seize the moments as they arise. If the kids go out for pizza, drop everything else and run to the bedroom! The chores, bill paying, and emails can wait until they get back.

When James turned thirty-nine, I hid thirty-nine slips of paper around the house. Each slip had something I appreciated about him written on it. Most of the comments were G-rated and just a few were about romantic love. I thought he had found all thirty-nine, but at his birthday party, our friend's young daughter asked her mom, "What's this?" She was holding a slip of paper that read, "I love the way you make me feel when we make love." Oops, that was embarrassing! Sometimes the messages we intend to be private get into the wrong hands. But that doesn't mean we should stop writing love notes.

Perhaps one of the greatest love notes of all time is open for all to read. Song of Songs 1:2,4 teaches us to seize the moment:

> Let him kiss me with the kisses of his mouth—
>   for your love is more delightful than wine…
> Take me away with you—let us hurry!
> Let the king bring me into his chambers.

Can you hear the joy in the Shulamite woman's voice? You can almost hear her giggling.

So the next time your husband suggests you put the dishes aside for something more romantic, remember to giggle and hurry up. You might also want to grab your salad kit on the way to the bedroom.

Today's Picture

Envision your handsome husband walking slowly toward you. He leans into you and whispers in your ear how much he loves you. You can't wait to fall into his embrace later in the evening because_____ (finish the sentence yourself).

Today's Prayer

Lord, I thank You for the beauty and intimacy of sexual love. I want to grow closer to my husband physically and enjoy the very best You have for both of us. Carve out pockets of time this week for my husband and me to be together. Take away anything that threatens to come between us. Make us one in body, mind, and spirit. Please put a passion for my husband deep in my heart.

Day 12

The Rest Challenged

"Come to me, all you who are weary and burdened,
and I will give you rest."

MATTHEW 11:28

Maybe you think, *I could be a happy wife if I weren't so tired.* When you are exhausted, ragged, run-down, and depleted, acting happy doesn't rise to the top of the to-do list. I totally get that. James would be the first to tell you that if sleeping were an Olympic sport, I'd have a shot at gold.

When I'm tired and worn-out, I am irritable. A routine task like returning a phone call seems monumental. In times like these, James has told me more than once, "You need to take a nap. *Please* go take a nap." Instead of being offended, I thankfully retire to my bedroom and lie down. I know that even ten minutes curled up in bed makes me a much nicer person for the remainder of the day (I'm even nicer after thirty minutes).

Sleeping Beauty

Like many of us, Pam Farrel wrestles with making time for rest. As a go-getter speaker and author, Pam tends to burn the candle at both ends. At an appointment, she asked her doctor why she wasn't losing weight. She had been exercising and eating healthy, and she didn't understand why she wasn't seeing results on the scale.

> One of the first questions my doctor asked me was about my sleep patterns. I answered, "I don't have many! I don't sleep enough. I go to bed after midnight and get up after sunrise."

The doctor said that waking after sunrise was good, but going to bed at midnight was not. Everyone needs seven to eight hours of sleep at minimum to maintain health. I had to reset my body clock and give myself permission to go to bed earlier.

When you have a good night's sleep, problems stay in their right perspective. When you're sleep deprived, every problem seems insurmountable. It's so easy to feel overwhelmed when you're not rested. I think when we give ourselves permission to take really good care of ourselves, we're just happier people. One of the best gifts we can give to ourselves is permission to take a twenty-minute nap in the middle of the afternoon if we need it to keep going. When I get enough sleep, I'm more focused. My mind is sharper. I don't have as many relationship issues because I'm nicer. I don't spend all my time solving arguments that I started![14]

Busy Is Overrated

I have an extremely fit friend who's a personal trainer. Just looking at her muscles you know she's got one thing many of us lack: self-discipline. Yet I heard her comment, "There is never enough time in the day!" Even the most disciplined among us can feel the stress of too much to do in too little time. High stress levels in women can lead to a rise in cortisol, which over time increases the risk for developing diabetes, heart disease, depression, fatigue, and obesity.

Dr. Sherita Hill Golden of the Johns Hopkins School of Medicine says, "Women are actually not articulating stress to their physicians because they're thinking this is just a normal way of functioning."[15] Look at your life and the lives of your friends. What's considered a normal schedule? Having your life scheduled from the time you wake up to the time you lie down is normal for many wives. There's no such thing as downtime anymore. Every minute is committed to some kind of activity: working, checking emails, texting, driving kids to school and sports, volunteering at church, getting an advanced degree, exercising, home decorating, and more. A busy schedule is a status symbol of success. You must be heading somewhere if you're as stressed out as everyone else.

In order to be a happy wife, you need to objectively examine your schedule. Do you have margin in your calendar or is every single hour accounted for? In his book *Margin: Restoring Emotional, Physical, Financial, and Time Reserves to Overloaded Lives*, Dr. Richard Swenson makes the comparison between a life with and without margins:

> Marginless is not having time to finish the book you're reading on stress; margin is having the time to read it twice.
> Marginless is fatigue; margin is energy.
> Marginless is red ink; margin is black ink.
> Marginless is hurry; margin is calm.
> Marginless is anxiety; margin is security.
> Marginless is culture; margin is counterculture.
> Marginless is the disease of the new millennium; margin is its cure. [16]

Many of us feel obligated to be busy, overcommitted, multitasking, ever-achieving women. We complain about not having enough time in the day, but we're unwilling to make any changes to our crazy lives. Consider what Zig Ziglar said, "Lack of direction, not lack of time, is the problem. We all have twenty-four-hour days." [17] No matter how hard you try, you can't do one thing to change the amount of time you're given in a day. But you can certainly change the way you choose to fill that time.

My friend, author Leeana Tankersley, is married to a Navy SEAL. She blogged this about slowing down:

> When you are drawing your weapon for the purposes of clearing a room, a SEAL will tell you, "Slow is smooth; smooth is fast." In other words, if you try to draw your weapon too quickly, chances are, in your attempt to be fast, you'll fumble or drop or mishandle the thing your very life depends on. But if you can focus on slow, deliberate movements, then your smoothness will translate to getting the job done faster and safer.
>
> Now I have absolutely no occasion to draw a weapon. None whatsoever. But, here's where this SEAL-ism hits home for me. I can tend to think that frenetic and frenzied and crazy-brained is how I must live to keep up with this world, technology, my schedule, others' expectations of me, etc. What if approaching life with deliberate calm, a sense of intention, and measured movements would, in the end, yield greater productivity and efficiency? [18]

Know Thyself

Here are a few questions to help you take inventory of your life and need for rest:

- What activities in your weekly schedule reflect your values (family relationships, work, health, finances, service, etc.)?

- What extras are taking up your time each week?

- What could you cut out or simplify to make more time for rest?

- How do you like to rest and get recharged (nap, watching a movie, bath, walk, journal)?

- Do you work best at a fast pace or a slower pace of life?

- Are you getting seven to eight hours of sleep every night?

- Do you exercise for one hour at least three times a week or every day for thirty minutes?

You might wonder what exercise has to do with rest. When you're tired, your natural instinct is not to go to the gym. Yet regular exercise will help you sleep more soundly and give you an energy boost during the day. In *31 Days to a Younger You* I wrote about going to spin class with my mother. We've been on hiatus for a few years and just started back up again. It feels great!

So if you wish you were a more rested wife, you might consider a new exercise routine or cutting out miscellaneous activities that are draining your energy with very little payback. And while you're looking at your calendar, why not plan a cozy Sunday afternoon nap for this weekend?

Today's Picture

If your weekly schedule were represented by a page in a book, what would it look like? Would it have structure or would it be scribbled all over? What about white space—would there be any margin or would every space be filled with activities?

Today's Prayer

Lord, I don't want to be so busy that I miss Your voice. I don't want to be so frazzled that I can't enjoy my life and my marriage. Show me how to slow down and make room for You to speak to me. Jesus, You call the weary and offer them rest. Help me to discern what's important in my schedule and what should be eliminated. Please give me rest and restore my soul.

HOPEFUL

ADAPTABLE

Becoming POSITIVE

P

Y

It's Lonely at the Top

How happy are those who reside in Your house,
who praise You continually.

PSALM 84:4 (HCSB)

Picture a group of five wives sitting in a coffee shop, chatting about their marriages. You hear one of them exclaim, "You wouldn't believe what my husband did yesterday!"

Usually what follows is a blow-by-blow recounting of something foolish that husband did or said. He forgot their anniversary or shrunk her favorite shirt in the dryer. Rarely is it something positive or praiseworthy. It's become popular sport to rant and rave about the shortcomings of our spouses and our lives.

Nowadays women bond through complaining with one another, commiserating over their second-class marriages and insensitive husbands. Complaining is justified because it's seen as therapeutic. We complain in order to know we're not alone. Underneath the nitpicking, there's a need to connect with others and to draw attention to oneself.

On the other hand, if you're a wife who's constantly raving about your husband, your friends might be busy the next time you call for coffee. A wife who's that happy has to be fake, spoiled, or prideful. Being a positive wife can alienate certain friends. The top of the world can be a lonely place.

The Hair Appointment That Changed Her Life

Fawn Weaver, author of *The Happy Wives Club,* was a young, successful business manager and co-owner of a fine-dining restaurant between

Beverly Hills and West Los Angeles. Although she dreamed of getting married, she didn't have time to mess around with dating and boyfriends. She was waiting for God to bring the right man to her.

She needed a new hairdresser, and her friend suggested a woman named Odia who had done her hair for more than fifteen years. Fawn ended up becoming one of Odia's customers, but unlike other clients, Fawn didn't like to talk in the salon. She was either dealing with staff on the phone or craving silence. Odia, however, kept the conversation usually centered on her favorite subject: her only child, a son who just happened to be single. Fawn remembers,

> One day she was washing my hair and said, "It's amazing at your age the level of business you conduct. I can't imagine where you'll be in your forties. You'll be ruling the world." To which I replied, "This is just a pastime. What I've always desired more is to be an excellent wife and mom." Not a full second later, Odia said, "You've got to meet my son!"
>
> She had her son, Keith, so high on a pedestal. I didn't want to meet anyone's only son!

Hair appointment after hair appointment, Fawn kept ignoring Odia's pleas to meet her son. Finally she relented and gave Odia her phone number. But after all that, Keith never called. Now it was Odia's turn to make excuses. *My son wants to call you but he's been so busy.*

Weeks passed and Fawn was really fine with it. She was attending a conference and was in her hotel room watching football in-between sessions. The phone rang and a man with a super-deep voice asked for her by name. "Is this the second coming?" Fawn joked. They both started laughing, and he said, "You've been speaking to my mother."

That first phone call lasted for hours. At the end of it, Fawn said to Keith,

> "This has been a great conversation. But if you wake up in the morning and you feel that you don't want to call me, listen to that voice. I have long prayed for the Lord to close the door to anyone who's not supposed to be my husband. I'm too busy to mess around." And that's how I ended the call!

Undaunted, Keith did call back, and they continued to talk by phone for several weeks. They scheduled their first date for May 9. The day before, Fawn came down with the stomach flu, but she was determined not to cancel the date.

> When Keith arrived and I opened the door, he will tell you to this day that I was the most beautiful woman he had ever seen. I was a little thinner than usual! I couldn't eat at dinner, but we had a wonderful date and we both knew then we would be married. There was no question about it.

They have been inseparable since that date. On September 6, he proposed, and on December 27, they eloped. They were planning a wedding in April, but the day after Christmas, Keith asked, "What's the reason we're waiting to get married? Why don't we get married tonight?" They drove to Las Vegas, and the following morning they were husband and wife.

Keith and Fawn didn't meet or marry in a conventional way. And compared to many couples, they don't really view marriage in a conventional way either. Fawn says,

> Many times, especially in the church, we hope to prepare married couples by giving them all these negative scenarios to look for. And if you look for something, you will find it every time. People would tell me, "You're going to argue." I would say, "That's your life, not mine." I would flat out reject those comments and be on a mission to prove them wrong.
>
> I purposed from the very beginning I would only listen to people who had positive things to say about marriage and who were already successful in their own marriage. And if I listened to people who were not successful in their marriage, it was only for the purpose of seeing what I should not do. I am counterculture all the way. It can be really beneficial to be rebellious!
>
> I think we should give people permission to be happy. It's something that's missing today because you don't want to boast. You can talk about how your husband never puts down the toilet seat, and no one will say anything. But if you talk about how he's considerate and always puts the roll of toilet paper the way you want it, now you're boasting. I think that should change. [1]

I agree with Fawn. Let us not be afraid to say it out loud: "My husband puts the toilet paper how I want it and I think he's wonderful!" Calling all rebels…it's time to be positive about our marriages. It doesn't have to be lonely at the top.

I love what Gary Chapman writes about the pivotal power of a positive attitude:

> Attitude has to do with the way I choose to think about things. It results from my focus. Two men looked through prison bars— one saw mud, the other stars. Two people were in a troubled marriage—one cursed, the other prayed. The difference is attitude.
>
> Negative thinking tends to beget more negative thinking. Focus on how terrible the situation is, and it will begin to seem even worse. Focus on one positive thing, and another will appear. In the darkest night of a troubled marriage, there is always a flickering light. Focus on that light, and it will eventually flood the room. [2]

Here's to flooding your home with light. Even the smallest flickering flame—a small positive change in attitude and actions—makes a big difference.

Today's Picture

You are standing on the top of a mountain. Your heart is full of love for your husband. You're so grateful that God has brought him into your life. What are you going to shout out to the world below? I love my husband because he is_____.

Today's Prayer

Lord, I want to focus on the stars and not the mud. I ask You to make me a more positive, joyful, and thankful person. Thank You for bringing my husband and me together. Continue to write our love story so that it brings glory and honor to You. Thank You, Jesus, that You are the light of the world. Come and fill my home and marriage with Your light.

Put Your Weapon Down

The tongue has the power of life and death,
and those who love it will eat its fruit.

PROVERBS 18:21

Just a few days before my fortieth birthday, James started making little comments that were getting under my skin. They weren't even about getting older. We were both feeling under the weather, but he would say things like, "You're not as sick as I am," and "Get up and go to the gym." He would criticize my driving (I'm sure that's never happened to you) saying, "Why are you accelerating to the red light? You should anticipate what's ahead on the road." After breakfast, he made a sarcastic remark about the messy table.

Can you feel the tension mounting? Even though many of his comments were made lightly, they were driving me crazy. I teased him back and asked him not to criticize me for a few days. He said with a smile that it was his gift to see areas that needed improvement.

When I was by myself, I realized that while my husband's words were hurtful, my reaction to them was complicating the issue. I prayed, *God, change me. Help me to like my husband right now. Help me not to be resentful. Help me to communicate to him the things that bother me and then help me forget about it.*

God answered my prayer that day. I realized afterward that if I kept a soft heart toward God, it would result in me having a soft heart toward my husband too. The reverse is also true. When I harden my heart toward my husband, I am also hardening my heart toward God. Our heart and our words are connected, as it says in Psalm 19:14,

May these words of my mouth and this meditation of my heart
   be pleasing in your sight,
LORD, my Rock and my Redeemer.

Will we use our words as weapons against our husbands to retaliate?
Or will we use our words to heal and restore?

My Mouth Keeps Getting Me in Trouble

Remember British author Poppy Smith and her story about regretting
her marriage to the dreamy American? She came to a crisis in her third or
fourth year of marriage and prayed to God about one of her biggest problems: her mouth.

> I began to ask God to show me when I was getting irritable
> because a lot of my problem was my mouth. My mother was very
> warm, spontaneous, emotional, and very verbal. Of course that
> is how I was. I had a real problem with getting irritable and los-
> ing my temper. I got angry before I was even aware of it. Bit by
> bit, the Lord was trying to show me that I was getting irritable. I
> could tell in my mind and in my body that I was tense.
>
> And the Holy Spirit would bring these thoughts to me: *Poppy,
> zip your lip!* If you don't say it, you cut so much pain out instead
> of stabbing each other with words. *Zip your lips.* Then the Lord
> unfolded this to me: *Turn your stumbling blocks into stepping-
> stones.* I would go to the bathroom, close the door, and just cry
> out to God. Physically our adrenaline gets going and perhaps
> that's what propels us to say things when we're upset. We need
> to get out of that situation. Maybe to go for a walk or to a quiet
> place and ask, *Okay Lord, what triggered my anger?*

Poppy wanted to learn where her unhappiness was coming from. She
didn't want to be like a hamster running, running, running on a wheel but
going nowhere. That's how she viewed her emotional responses to her husband. As she began to ask herself, "How do I build my marriage instead
of destroying it?" she saw that she did have the power and control of the
Holy Spirit over her heart and mouth. Gradually Poppy began to change.

> After being too verbal, I swung the other way and stuffed it. I
> just wouldn't say anything. I wanted to only take it to the Lord.

But then I wasn't building the relationship. I was allowing a lot of anger to build in me. I wasn't saying anything, but it was there.

I learned how to speak up and not to bury it. *When you just said that, I felt this. Is that what you meant?* I think about what my words are doing. Am I diminishing or devaluing him? Is he doing that to me? We've learned to say to each other, *I'm sorry, I didn't mean that. That wasn't what I intended to say.* Now we build bonds together. We still get irritated with each other because we see things in different ways. But we want our marriage to continue and to be happy for both of us. We need to find ways to cooperate and work together. [3]

Sticks and Stones

We can learn so much from Poppy's story. It's possible to change deeply ingrained habits, especially with the power of the Holy Spirit. If you have a history of talking back to your husband in anger, you don't have to live enslaved to outbursts. You don't want to stuff your feelings, but you do want to learn how to communicate in a constructive, not a destructive, way. How can you tell the difference? Let's say you want to tell your husband you were upset by the way he brushed off your comment about purchasing a large item.

Constructive words: "Honey, I am trying to be more responsible with money. But it didn't even seem like you were listening to my concerns. Is there a better time for us to talk? Do you disagree with what I said?"

Destructive words: "I don't know why I bother to try to reason with you. When I have an opinion, you just shut me down. You don't care about what I think about our finances. You make decisions without considering my feelings all the time."

Can you see how your words set the stage for your husband's response? Constructive words look for a solution. They seek to improve things and promote growth. They are useful and helpful. Keep in mind that constructive words can be negative. Many times you have to diagnose and talk about a problem honestly before you can fix it.

Destructive words act as the opposite. They seek to damage, discredit, and ruin. They are always unfavorable and negative. There's nothing redemptive about destructive words. They lodge in our hearts and cause long-term harm if woefully unattended. We all know the saying "Sticks and stones may break my bones, but words will never hurt me" is untrue.

Proverbs 19:13 says that "a quarrelsome wife is like the constant dripping of a leaky roof." We want to be roof repairers and not constant drippers. We want our words to cause growth in our marriages and not ruin. Today is a great day to put down our sticks, stones, and hurtful words.

Today's Picture

When you open your mouth to speak to your husband, what kind of words usually come out? Are they positive words like a bouquet of flowers? Or are they sharp words, more like sticks and stones?

Today's Prayer

Lord, may the meditation of my heart and the words of my mouth be pleasing to You. Forgive me for being a quarrelsome wife. Help me to seek peace and to use my words in a constructive, affirming way. Give me the right words to say to my husband today. Fill me with the Holy Spirit so that I can exercise self-control every day with my words.

From Bothers to Blessings

All the days of the oppressed are wretched,
but the cheerful heart has a continual feast.

PROVERBS 15:15

What bugs you most about being a wife? Maybe it's dealing with your husband's crazy work schedule or those dratted socks on the floor. Today we're going to consider how to change *bothers* into *blessings*. You face a choice every day. Will you be irritated or grateful for your husband as a package deal with all his strengths and weaknesses?

Pam Farrel keeps nagging to a minimum at her house by focusing on her husband's integrity. She's extremely grateful that Bill keeps his promises to her and the kids. He's faithful to God. With that in mind, picking up his dirty coffee cups from all around the house isn't so bad.

But what if your husband hasn't been keeping his promises lately? If he's failing in a major area, such as addiction or an affair, I suggest you go to a Christian counselor. You having a positive attitude will help, but it will not solve the root problem. Glossing over what is wrong will not help anyone. But if he's not engaged in destructive behavior, you would be wise to focus on his strengths and not his warts.

It's So Easy to Complain

There is a palpable difference between complaining and constructive criticism. Let's say you text your husband a shopping list for the grocery store. When he gets home, you realize that he has forgotten to buy the chicken. *How are you supposed to make the meal without chicken? You texted him the list clearly. How could he be so careless?* He apologizes and says he just missed reading that all-important word *chicken*. You eat leftovers.

The next day, you're having lunch with your girlfriends. "You know what my husband did yesterday?" you ask. "I texted him a shopping list for dinner, and he forgot to bring home the chicken. How in the world can you miss something so basic?"

Your friend chimes in about how she never trusts her husband with the shopping list. Another wife says you should be glad your husband actually goes to the store because her husband won't. You haven't even ordered lunch yet, and the complaining locomotive is picking up steam.

Many wives believe the lie that complaining is okay because it's a form of venting. But venting (giving expression to something) is helpful only when it's done with the appropriate people and with a positive purpose of redemption. Most venting is complaining, grumbling, whining, and lamenting renamed. It's not constructive. It doesn't bring you closer to your spouse. It's marvelous at doing the opposite—driving a wedge between you.

On the other hand, constructive criticism about the forgotten chicken would be directed toward your spouse, not your friends. You want to make comments that are actually useful and intended to improve the situation. "Honey, next time you do the shopping, can you slow down and make sure that every item is in the cart before you check out? Would you prefer me to email you a list? Can you go back to the store now and get the chicken?" Work on solving the problem, not attacking the wrongdoer. The chicken dilemma should be taken care of at home. Then there would be no more chicken left to complain about the next day at lunch with friends.

Talk Him Up

Kathi Lipp addresses the importance of talking up your husband with friends instead of tearing him down:

> If you are talking down your husband to me and you're not doing anything to correct your relationship, I love you, I care about you, but I can't hang out with you. Because the expectation is you want me to talk down my husband as well. And I'm not going to do that. I have been in a relationship like that before and the temptation is to be with the crowd.

I heard once that you become like the five people you most hang out with. That is so wise. If the people I hang out with are negative toward their husbands, I will be negative about my husband. But if they are committed to building into their marriage and their husband, I am going to be the same way.

Find things on purpose to respect your husband about. Even if the only thing you can say to him is *Thank you for making the bed six months ago when your mom came.* If that's all you've got, start with that. Because the more you look for those things to encourage him about, the more you'll find other positive things. Plus it's amazing how much nicer husbands can be when we're nice. It makes such a huge difference.

Kathi suggests getting together with a girlfriend not to complain about your marriage but to ask each other, "What have you said to encourage your husband today?"

If your husband isn't acting in a way that's connecting to you, sometimes it's not about you. He's feeling like a loser at work or a loser as a parent. There are so many truths that only a wife can speak into her husband. Being able to say *I love you, I care about you, I think you're so smart, I miss you, you make me feel protected,* these are things that can change your husband. And in so doing, you change your own satisfaction level in the marriage. [4]

The Trouble with Grumbles

What was one of the major sins the children of Israel committed after escaping from Egypt? It was the sin of complaining. They grumbled about what they would drink (Exodus 15:24; 17:3), about what they would eat (Exodus 16:3), and about dying in the wilderness (Numbers 14:2).

The LORD said to Moses and Aaron, "How long will this wicked community grumble against me? I have heard the complaints of these grumbling Israelites. So tell them, 'As surely as I live, declares the LORD, I will do to you the very thing I heard you say: In this wilderness your bodies will fall—every one of you twenty years old or more who was counted in the census and who has grumbled against me'" (Numbers 14:26-29).

Grumbling literally became a death sentence for the people of Israel. The evil power of complaining cannot be underestimated. The opposite of complaining is rejoicing. Instead of grumbling or protesting against something, you are finding reasons for joy. Sharon Jaynes suggests: "Today make a commitment to turn your grumbling to grateful, your complaining into contentment, and your whining into praising God." [5]

In a marriage, when you choose to thank God for your husband daily, there will be no room for grumbling. You will overlook those little things that used to bother you, choosing to home in on the many things you are thankful for. A grateful heart, unlike the grumbling heart, welcomes God's presence in your home, turning your wilderness into a spring of life. Zig Ziglar said it so well, "The more you are grateful for what you have, the more you will have to be grateful for." [6]

Today's Picture

You are holding a magnifying glass. Instead of zeroing in on your husband's faults, you are going to intentionally place that magnifying glass right over his strengths. What are two strengths that you see?

Today's Prayer

Lord, I repent of complaining about my husband and grumbling about my life. I want to give You praise for blessing me with _____ and _____. Thank You for the strength that my husband brings to our marriage. Thank You for his wisdom and integrity. Bless my husband and me with a close, encouraging relationship that brings honor to You.

Smile, Not Just for the Camera

But let all who take refuge in you be glad;
let them ever sing for joy...
Surely, LORD, you bless the righteous;
you surround them with your favor as with a shield.

PSALM 5:11,12

When someone points a camera your way, what do you do? I hope you smile! Chances are your husband loves to see that smile, not just for the camera but throughout the day. Liz Curtis Higgs says her husband tells her often how much he loves her smile. He says when she smiles, it's like sunshine. Liz says,

> Maybe I need to make sure the sun is shining a lot! As we go about our day, we're often not smiling. It's not that we're frowning. We're just preoccupied. I sometimes see candid pictures of me, and the look on my face is not a happy look. It's not grumpy; it's just sort of flat. Like my brain is running and my face forgets to be happy. And scientists say that smiling itself improves your attitude. [7]

Researchers are finding that wearing a smile brings certain health benefits. A study that involved 170 participants got people to smile by making them hold a pair of chopsticks in three different ways in their mouth. One way forced people to have a neutral expression, the second way caused a polite smile, and the third forced a full smile that involved the muscles around the mouth and eyes. The smiling participants recovered from physiological stress faster and had slower heart rates. [8]

Try This at Breakfast

One of my favorite books is Dale Carnegie's classic *How to Win Friends and Influence People*. As a part of his human relations courses, he asked business people to smile at someone every hour of the day for a week and then come to class to talk about the results. One New York stockbroker wrote Mr. Carnegie a letter about how he had been married eighteen years, yet seldom smiled at his wife or spoke to her before leaving for work. He was one of the worst grouches to walk down Wall Street.

> When you asked me to make a talk about my experience with smiles, I thought I would try it for a week. So the next morning, while combing my hair, I looked at my glum mug in the mirror and said to myself, "Bill, you are going to wipe the scowl off that sour puss of yours today. You are going to smile. And you are going to begin right now." As I sat down to breakfast, I greeted my wife with a "Good morning, my dear," and smiled as I said it.
>
> You warned me that she might be surprised. Well, you underestimated her reaction. She was bewildered. She was shocked. I told her in the future she could expect this as a regular occurrence, and I kept it up every morning. This changed attitude of mine brought more happiness into our home in the last two months since I started than there was during the last year. [9]

Can you imagine being that wife and what it would mean to you if your grouchy husband transformed into a smiling breakfast companion? You may not be half as grouchy as this husband, but perhaps you could benefit from having a morning pep talk to tell your face to smile.

Liz Curtis Higgs uses red lipstick to tell her face to smile. "I always wear bright red lipstick," she says. "I have always worn it when it was cool and when it wasn't cool." When she gets out her mirror for touch-ups throughout the day, she smiles as she applies her lipstick. Red lipstick makes her feel dressier, zippier, and happier—plus it reminds her to smile and let the sun shine. [10]

But He Doesn't Give Me a Reason to Smile

What if you want your husband to make you smile, but he isn't giving you much to work with? I remember a very busy Wednesday in our home.

First, I woke up at 5:30 a.m. for boot camp at the gym. James will tell you it is unusual for me to get up that early (remember my love for sleep?). Then I headed to the kids' elementary school to watch Ethan's class participate in a folk-dancing festival followed by refreshments in the classroom. I rushed home and had a radio interview and then needed to update my website, which was being redesigned. Plus I had speaking engagements to prepare for the next few days. And did I mention we were having company stay at our house the following day, so I needed to clean.

Have you ever had one of those days?

I was feeling the need for some serious words of affirmation from James. But, of course, I didn't tell him that. I was dropping hints left and right, but he was not catching on. I'm huffing and puffing, walking quickly around the house with cleaning supplies. I'm sighing and talking about how much I had to do. I'm waiting for a comforting word or a compliment. He continues working from his office in silence.

Now I'm even more stressed out because I've added "I have an insensitive husband" to my list of grievances. Then it hits me. I am just doing my job. Why am I trying to get extra attention? As a mother, author, and speaker, these are the kinds of activities that are part of the package. I don't commend James every time he takes the kids to school, completes his business calls, and texts his clients. That's all part of his job. That evening, I wrote this in my journal:

> I realized today that I need to do my part and not wait for the kudos. Instead of thinking James will meet all my needs for affirmation, I need to lean on the Lord more for validation. I want to stop waiting for him to say the magic words. The truth is, he doesn't even know he's supposed to say them.

There will be many times when your husband will do or say something that will bring a big smile to your face. But don't count on your husband to be the main source of your smile. He simply can't live up to that. And when you need those words of affirmation, ask for them. Remember, your husband is not a mind reader.

I interviewed *Focus on the Family* cohost John Fuller for my book *31 Days to a Happy Husband*. This time around I had the joy of talking to his wife, Dena. They have six children, and Dena, like most of us, finds it a struggle from time to time to keep smiling.

We have a lot of humor in our home, and it puts things in perspective. Depending on the night around the kitchen table, we might be in tears laughing or having an argument between teenage girls that has me going to my bedroom in tears. But levity is very important. You have to be able to laugh about things that at first may not make you laugh.

Putting that smile on my face is about looking to Jesus and finding smiles in the small moments in the day. Sometimes I'm okay at that. Sometimes I fail miserably. His mercies are new every morning, so you just keep at it.

There's emotional pain in this world. Joy has to be alongside that. I don't think the joy takes away the pain. You can have grief on one track and joy on the other. Those two emotions can be running together at the same time. [11]

Just because you have a smile on your face doesn't mean that every single thing is perfect in your life. But it can be a physical expression to demonstrate your faith in God. Rejoice and give your smile away. Your husband may really need to see the sun shine through you. Here's a beautiful reminder of the value of a smile:

It costs nothing, but creates much.
It enriches those who receive it without impoverishing those who give it.
It happens in a flash, and the memory of it sometimes lasts forever. [12]

Today's Picture

Picture your face—you are smiling broadly. Now picture yourself frowning. Next picture your face with that blah, neutral expression. Lastly, picture your face with a small smile on your lips. You look and feel better with a smile on your face, don't you? Today you are going to frown less. When you see your husband, you will smile. Let the sun shine.

Today's Prayer

Lord, You say that a merry heart is like medicine. Smiling is good for my health. Help me to smile more often. I give You my worries and concerns. I give my burdens to You because I know You care for me. I choose to smile because I know I am loved. Thank You for loving me.

It's Easy Being Married to You

When she speaks she has something worthwhile to say,
and she always says it kindly.

PROVERBS 31:26 (MSG)

L ast year, James and I did a Daniel fast. [13] He had lost five pounds and I had lost a pathetic half pound. As he teased me, I defended myself by declaring, "I'm not doing it to lose weight. I'm doing it as unto God!" To be honest, I *was* trying to lose weight, but it felt good to rationalize. I began stewing in my mind. *James is too focused on weight. He's obsessed. He's so demanding.*

I felt hurt, and I didn't want that frustration to fester. So I brought it up, and he was gracious. The talk was going very well until he confessed that he agreed to do the fast with me to help me lose weight. He meant it as something nice (think of all the husbands who won't give up junk food even when their wives are trying to diet), but I heard it as, "I just did this fast to help you get skinnier, because let's face it, you have some weight to lose."

I did not think it was easy being married to James at that moment. (Keep in mind that we are fasting, and here we are arguing!) After a while, we weren't even sure what we were fighting about. We both concluded that we were under spiritual attack, so we prayed together.

James disappeared, and I heard the garage door open. I thought he was sneaking out to buy me flowers. But a few minutes later, he came in the room holding our box full of love letters from when we were dating, engaged, and newly married. He asked me to pull out three random letters to read together. One of the letters was from our first months of marriage. It was my response to a question he had written, "What do I do that pushes your buttons and irritates you?" I had written two things:

- Leave me alone (don't try to improve me).
- Don't think because it's easy for you, it's easy for me (for example, last-minute entertaining).

It was divinely funny! Here we were, more than a decade later, and those two things still were bothering me. I wanted James to leave me alone about my weight, and I was mad that losing five pounds was easy for him but not for me. You can see how the Holy Spirit led me to pick that exact letter out of more than one hundred notes.

I want to add, before you think too critically of my James and his comments about my weight, this is the husband who asked his new bride, "Tell me about the things I do that bother you. I want to be aware of those things and do my best not to offend you." Now that's someone who's easy to be married to.

Since you live with your spouse, it's inevitable that you will butt heads, step on each other's toes, and rub each other the wrong way. But I have found it so helpful to replace the mind-set of "you are so difficult to live with" to "it's easy being married to you."

But I Don't Even Like Him

Maybe you can relate to this account of two friends talking:

Melba: My husband was named Man of the Year.

Pam: Well, that shows you what kind of a year it's been. [14]

Your husband might not be on your top ten list of favorite people every day of the year. Keep in mind you may not be on his list year round either. If you dwell on the things you don't like about your husband, your dissatisfaction will grow and turn you into one very unhappy wife.

Leslie Vernick says:

> Often we're hoping for the wrong thing. We're hoping for Prince Charming. When we have these unrealistic Hollywood or Harlequin expectations of marriage, we can become disillusioned because nobody can live up to that.

I often see marriages that are very unhappy. Sometimes a woman is in a C-minus marriage. But then because she is so disappointed, she makes it a D marriage. Every marriage has its disappointments, so how are you handling those disappointments? [15]

When we make our disappointments larger than life and rehearse them over and over, we can't appreciate the good husbands we have. Pam Farrel says,

> The number one thing I see in our marriage ministry is really good men being criticized by their wives. I will meet with a woman, and she'll say, "My husband works so much. He doesn't have time for me. He watches TV." I want to say, "Look around, your husband has a job when a lot of men don't. Wow, he's a really good dad. He's a leader and volunteer at church." It's easy for women to nitpick on really good men rather than stepping back and saying, "Wow, I am so fortunate. My husband doesn't beat me, he doesn't come home drunk all the time, he isn't cheating on me with other women." If you're married to a normal guy, maybe he is a little bit boring and has just a regular job. I encourage you to look for the positive in that guy.
>
> Early in my marriage, I was complaining about my pastor husband not having enough time for me. I decided to take inventory and realized it was a privilege to be married to a very responsible man a lot of people wanted to spend time with. Maybe as wives, we will be happier if we start giving our husbands thanks and praise for the little things they do. [16]

The Art of Appreciation

Leadership experts Ken and Marjorie Blanchard were hosting a reunion for Marjorie's college sorority class. She noticed Ken out of the corner of her eye picking up dishes and cleaning up while she was busy talking with her friends. At the end of the evening, she walked into the kitchen and it was all cleaned up. The dishes were in the dishwasher and the trash had been taken out. She thought to herself, *That's great! What a nice guy my husband is!* But she forgot to say anything to Ken.

I went upstairs to bed. Ken says to me, "You know, I'm kind

of sitting here waiting for a praising." Right away, I thought I should have said something, but I had forgotten about it. I thought it was wonderful that he asked me for the praise.

Ken is absolutely right when he says that the healthiest relationships have four times as many praises as criticisms. If we can appreciate what each other is doing and be very generous with appreciation, we always have something in the relational bank to draw out. [17]

What are the things you love and appreciate about your husband? You can start a running list of reasons why it's easy to love him. Here's the start of mine. It's easy to love James because:

- He's a man of integrity who keeps his word.

- He laughs every day.

- He's a great listener and doesn't just endure our conversations; he actually enjoys them (or at least always gives me that impression!).

- He's a proactive father who believes it's his primary responsibility, not the schools' or anyone else's, to teach our kids life skills.

I'm just getting warmed up! Now it's your turn to think about why it's easy being married to your man. The more positive traits you look for, the more you will find.

Today's Picture

List three things that make it easy to be married to your husband:

1.

2.

3.

Today's Prayer

Lord, I know I can be difficult to live with sometimes. Thank You for the times my husband has been patient with me, and help me to be patient with him. Give me wisdom to appreciate my husband. Give me fresh eyes to see what makes my husband truly great. Thank You that I get to live my life alongside this awesome man. You have been so good to us.

Case Dismissed

A person's wisdom yields patience;
it is to one's glory to overlook an offense.

PROVERBS 19:11

I remember the first fight James and I had as newlyweds. I was not a good cook, but I had acquired a secret weapon to aid my culinary cause: a brand-new George Foreman grill. It looked easy enough—place the chicken in, close the lid, and allow the patented sloped design and non-stick coating to do the rest! I was going to make chicken, rice, and broccoli. This was a big event in my new-bride life.

It was about 5:00 p.m. when James bounded into our small Dallas apartment on the fourth floor. "There's a guy I passed on the way up," he said. "He's just moving in. Why don't we invite him over for dinner?"

There was no way I was having a guest for dinner. First, I didn't have enough chicken for more than two people. Second, I was nervous about serving the dinner just to James, let alone a guest. Third, our apartment didn't have much furniture and was in no condition for entertaining. Fourth, I am a planner while James is spontaneous, and this was *not* planned.

I clearly outlined these reasons to James and apologized that we wouldn't be able to do it. I returned to slaving over my George Foreman grill. About ten minutes later, James waltzed in the kitchen and announced with a twinkle in his eye, "Our new neighbor, Walter, will be up for dinner in a few minutes."

Didn't I just say he couldn't come? I was fuming! After I slammed cabinet drawers shut and set up another place setting, the doorbell rang.

"Hello, Walter!" I said pleasantly.

During dinner, I ate very little chicken and broccoli as Walter enjoyed my share. Right after Walter left and the door was closed, my smile immediately turned into a scowl and I stomped into the kitchen.

James literally tackled me and threw me on the floor in Tigger-like fashion. He lay right on top of me and put his big grinning face close to mine and said emphatically, "I'm sorry!"

I said, "Are you sorry because I'm mad or are you sorry because what you did was wrong and you won't do it again?"

He paused to think about that. After more fuming and talking, he said he was truly sorry and that he would not do it again. I accepted his apology and am happy to say that he has never brought someone home for dinner against my will. Case dismissed! (And Walter, if you're out there somewhere, you're welcome to come for dinner as long as you give me advance notice.)

Grudge Be Gone

Two human beings who share life together are bound to disagree. In those moments, the happy wife does not seek to be right. She's not argumentative by nature. She doesn't automatically go on the attack. Instead, she seeks to resolve the matter at hand. She doesn't act only in her own best interests. She looks out for the interests of her husband and the marriage.

A church marquee read, "No matter how much you nurse a grudge, it won't get better." [18] When we have been offended, we can rehearse those words or that scene over and over in our minds. We can hold on to our hurts. They even prove handy when we need justification to retaliate or to act coldly toward our husbands. We can boast to others about how hard we have it and receive a sense of importance because of our emotional pain.

But the Bible makes it very clear that we are not to hold grudges. We are not to allow that bitter feeling of resentment to build and grow strong. The Lord's Prayer says, "And forgive us our debts, as we also have forgiven our debtors" (Matthew 6:12). As if that weren't enough, Jesus repeats it for emphasis in verses 14 and 15, "For if you forgive other people when they sin against you, your heavenly Father will also forgive you. But if you do not forgive others their sins, your Father will not forgive your sins."

The antidote to holding a grudge is to lavish forgiveness. When you're tempted to withhold forgiveness from your spouse, consider this observation from Sharon Jaynes:

> Every time Satan came to Jesus in the wilderness to tempt Him, Jesus didn't try to outmuscle him or outfight him; He just outtruthed him. And that's what we can do. Every time Satan comes at us with a lie, we recognize that lie, we reject that lie, and just like Jesus we say, "It is written." And we stand on that truth whether we feel like it or not. It has nothing to do with feelings. [19]

Satan may be feeding you lies about your husband. *He doesn't really love you. He never listens to you. He doesn't make you happy.* Instead of embracing these lies, respond with truth from God's Word: "Be kind and compassionate to one another, forgiving each other, just as in Christ God forgave you" (Ephesians 4:32).

Will This Matter Tomorrow?

When Diana Wallis Taylor and her husband are having any kind of conflict, she asks herself a simple clarifying question: *Is this worth making an issue of now and will it matter tomorrow?* This question gives her tremendous perspective. When you realize it's not a big issue that will matter in the future, it makes it easier to let go of your frustration. But if whatever is bugging you would matter tomorrow, then it is a bona fide conflict that needs to be dealt with at greater length.

Isn't that a great question? When you feel yourself getting upset at your spouse, ask yourself, *Will this really matter tomorrow?*

I had an immediate opportunity to test this advice just a few hours after Diana told it to me. My family went to our first rodeo, and at the gate, we were told to throw away all our food. A rules keeper, I immediately tossed my apple slices in the trash. James, however, pulled our family of five out of the line to quickly consume the snacks we had brought from home. He asked me for the apples.

"Um, I threw them away," I replied quietly.

"How could you throw away perfectly good food?" he said. "You know Pellicanes do not throw away perfectly good food. I was looking forward to eating those apples!"

"I didn't know we were going to eat outside the gate," I said. "I was just doing what the man said. It's not a big deal. Let's just get kettle corn."

Then I remembered Diana's advice and thought to myself, *This will not matter at all tomorrow.* It was over, and neither of us brought up the word *apple* for the rest of the evening (and the kettle corn was delicious).

It's much easier to be a positive wife when you're not holding any grudges. If you need help because you tend to keep a record of wrongs, try meditating on how love behaves:

> Love is patient, love is kind. It does not envy, it does not boast, it is not proud. It does not dishonor others, it is not self-seeking, it is not easily angered, it keeps no record of wrongs (1 Corinthians 13:4-5).

Today's Picture

You know how water just rolls off a duck's back? Picture the small things that irritate you about your husband just rolling off your back. Don't dwell on them. Don't make them bigger than they are.

Today's Prayer

Lord, the Bible says that love keeps no record of wrongs. I release any grudges I am holding against my husband. I choose to forgive my husband for past hurts. Set me free from unforgiveness. I don't want to be bogged down by bitterness and unforgiveness. You have forgiven me of my sins, and I understand I can draw on Your strength to forgive others. Fill me with Your grace today.

Focus 4

HOPEFUL

ADAPTABLE

POSITIVE

Becoming PURPOSEFUL

Y

The Professional Wife

Honor her for all that her hands have done,
and let her works bring her praise at the city gate.

PROVERBS 31:31

M y first job in high school was being a hostess at a 1950s style café. I got to wear saddle shoes and a black-and-white checkered poufy skirt. Although I loved that job, I knew I didn't want to be sixty years old and still seating parties of four there. I made plans to have a career in broadcasting.

What career plans have you made in your life? You've probably been intentional about attending classes, getting a college degree, or interning to learn a trade. You've done grunt work, asked questions, and worked your way up professionally. Women are naturally self-starters, go-getters, and multitaskers. When we've got our eye on something we want, we'll move heaven and earth to get there.

Let's transfer this strong work ethic to our marriages. Have you made any career plans as a wife? Do you have any goals to achieve in your marriage? Most of us don't approach marriage like this. We're intentional at work or in parenting, but when it comes to our marriages, we often let the chips fall where they may.

In the next few days, you'll be challenged to be more purposeful and professional as a wife. Treat your role as wife not as a dreaded job but as a promising career. What you're creating at home isn't akin to flipping burgers at the corner fast-food restaurant. It's more like being the vice president of a Fortune 500 company—although it may not feel like that on some days!

Seeking Virtuous Wives

You'll never find this job listing in the classifieds, but it's something greatly needed today in families—*Wanted: Virtuous Wives*. From ancient times, a woman of moral excellence has been hard to find. Proverbs 31:10 asks,

> A wife of noble character who can find?
> She is worth far more than rubies.

I was a guest in my son's third-grade class, and I read a story from William Bennett's *The Book of Virtues*. Imagine my surprise when I asked what a virtue was and no one except my son could answer that question. Kids aren't the only ones who don't ponder what it means to live a virtuous life. Virtue means moral excellence, right living, and goodness. Unfortunately, many marriages are more influenced by desperate housewives than virtuous ones.

So how can you plan on purpose to make virtue a vital part of your job description? Perhaps you can make it your first goal as a professional wife to read Proverbs 31:10-31 every night before you go to bed this week. In Proverbs 31, we can find many qualities of the virtuous wife. She is trustworthy, good, diligent, hardworking, responsible, charitable, wise, entrepreneurial, savvy, prepared, and she's even clothed in fine linen and purple. Matthew Henry's commentary says this about her relationship with her husband:

> He thinks himself so happy in her that he envies not those who have most of the wealth of this world; he needs it not, he has enough, having such a wife. Happy the couple that have such a satisfaction as this in each other![1]

100 Percent Wife

There are numerous songs, skits, blog posts, and even movies about the many hats we wear as women. We have a work hat, wife hat, parent hat, daughter hat, friend hat, volunteer hat. Sometimes we get confused and overwhelmed by the many responsibilities that tug at our time, attention, and affection.

Bethany Palmer can certainly relate to that. She's the president of

Envoy Financial, where her father serves as the CEO. She's co-CEO of The Money Couple with her husband, Scott. She works with her husband and father, and then has her roles as wife and mom to her two school-age children.

> Being that wife that you want to be really comes down to a decision every single day. When I get home, it's time to shift gears and focus on my husband. I want the house clean. Every day when he comes home, I want him to feel it's a special place to be. I give him a big kiss, because in our situation I just saw him two hours ago in the office, but this is the time for me to be a wife and to make the home a place where he is excited to come to. He kisses me before he greets the dog, and it's those little things that make you feel special. It's that conscious decision to take the joy I have in my heart and make him a happy husband. I take a minute before I put on that wife hat, and I breathe and ask how can I wear this hat in the best way possible today?
>
> Do I do that perfectly every day? Absolutely not. But something that has helped me is that conscious decision of knowing what hat I'm wearing and doing it the best that I can do and not worrying about the other hats while I'm wearing that one.

Isn't that a great perspective? When you are wearing your wife hat, be in that role 100 percent. Don't be distracted by other things when you have that precious time during the day to be a wife to your husband. Be intentional with that time together. Bethany continues,

> It's so easy to blur all your roles. When you need to be in the parent mode, you're talking to your husband about work. But the time to talk about that is when you and your husband are working together, not when you're in the parenting and kid mode. Understanding the hat and understanding the mode—I think that really brings happiness because we have to be intentional with our relationships. Our relationship with our husband is a relationship that we have to mold, massage, and protect or it just dwindles.
>
> We have to give our perfectionism over to God. We sometimes think we have to do it so perfectly, so we add all these additional commitments. The work and everything will be there tomorrow.

It's not going anywhere. Leave it at work. Leave it in those walls.
Let it go and wear your wife hat. [2]

But Wait, There's More

As you probably know from experience, anything carried to an extreme
can become problematic. If you are unmotivated, totally laid back, and
apathetic about your role as a wife, you're going to drift your way right
into marriage counseling. But if you find all your significance in your role
as a wife, that's not healthy either. One relationship alone cannot meet all
your emotional and spiritual needs. Leslie Vernick says about her husband,

> One of the things we do is we give each other a lot of respect and
> validation. "You have great strengths and I appreciate you." It's
> not all just about the marriage. We each have our own goals. I
> think that is so important in a healthy marriage. [3]

So it's healthy to have personal, business, financial, spiritual, and family goals. Just make sure in your next goal-setting time that you include a
few goals as a wife. What can you do to strengthen your marriage in the
next six months? Here are a few ideas to get you started:

- Pick up a hobby that you and your husband can enjoy
  together.

- Read a book to help you understand your man better.

- Serve together for charity.

- Pray together before bedtime.

- Make your husband's favorite meal.

- Participate in a sports event together, such as a walk, bike ride,
  or team sport.

Sometime today, hold a photograph of your husband and take ten sec-
onds to stare at his face. You made a vow to love, honor, and cherish him
all the days of your life. As you purpose to grow as a wife, you'll not only
have job security in the years ahead. You'll love every minute of your lifetime career and calling as a wife.

Today's Picture

If your husband had to write a job description for what he needed in a wife, what do you think would be three top qualities he would be looking for:

1.

2.

3.

If you dare, you can ask him this question later today and see how your answers correspond.

Today's Prayer

Lord, thank You that I am a wife. I am grateful to be married to my husband, and I want to better understand the important role I play in our home. I don't want to be passive about being a wife. I want to be intentional. Show me how to be productive and virtuous like the Proverbs 31 wife. Take me through it one step at a time so I won't be overwhelmed. Help me to manage my household with wisdom and grace.

Day 20

Intimacy by Design

Listen! My beloved!
Look! Here he comes,
leaping across the mountains,
bounding over the hills.

Song of Songs 2:8

Several years ago, I entered a video contest to win a free night stay at the Grand Hyatt in downtown San Diego. I unashamedly put my little kids up to acting in the video, and we won! Thanks to that contest, James and I spent our tenth wedding anniversary in a luxurious corner room on the twenty-third floor. Not only was the room lovely, the hotel sent up complimentary champagne, truffles, and chocolate-covered strawberries. When we looked out the window after dark, the downtown lights filled the night sky. It was utterly romantic and perfect.

As you and I know very well, not every evening of marriage is like this. But once in a while, you have to plan something special to look forward to—creating intimacy by design.

Not Much Time for Spontaneous

A healthy sexual relationship with your husband is an important part of being a happy wife. But in many marriages, intimacy takes a backseat to other priorities, such as carpooling kids to events, getting an advanced degree, or putting in overtime at work. Cliff and Joyce Penner, authors of *The Gift of Sex: A Guide to Sexual Fulfillment*, write that one of the greatest areas of frustration for a vast majority of people is finding time for sex.[4] Can you relate?

I'm a big believer in regularly scheduling romantic times with my husband. Even though *spontaneous* may sound dreamier, spontaneous just doesn't happen in most busy households. Most of us need to schedule in regular times for intimacy, date nights, and seasonal getaways. If physical closeness is a priority in your marriage, you and your husband must communicate often about sex.

If you're a night person, but he's got a project at work that leaves him exhausted by the time he gets home, what can you do? Maybe he likes to make love in the morning, but that isn't remotely appealing to you. Changing circumstances with work, children, or health will put different demands on your time and energy levels. You need to talk about solutions that work for both of you. You have the same goal—to make time for mutually satisfying love and physical affection—so remember you are on the same team as you talk.

Sometimes you go through very busy and unusually taxing seasons of life when regular sex is just not happening. One way to alleviate that stress for both of you is to schedule a weekend getaway. Within a few hours from where you live, there is most likely a quaint getaway or bustling city that would make an ideal vacation place for romance. But remember, you don't have to spend money on a weekend away if you don't want to. You could vacation at a local hotel or even stay home (as long as you disconnect from work and send your kids to a friend's house).

Reading Up

Once James made the comparison between me writing a book and lovemaking. He said that when I'm writing a book, I interview people and research my topic. I am focused. He challenged me to be that purposeful when it comes to sex. Could I read good books about sexuality and be purposeful in the bedroom? I must admit my initial reaction was to shirk back and think, *I don't need another thing to do*. But as I thought about it more, my attitude began to change.

So if you're looking for a good Christian book about sex, you can come borrow one from me. I have quite a collection now floating around my nightstand, such as *The Gift of Sex, Is That All He Thinks About?, The Husband Project*, and the list goes on. I want to be constantly learning about intimacy because I know it's important for my marriage.

In *Red-Hot Monogamy: Making Your Marriage Sizzle,* Bill and Pam Farrel write,

> A pleasant surprise to us is that when we make the goal of sex to emotionally connect with our mate and give him or her pleasure, the love boomerangs back around, and we discover something new that is fun or fulfilling to us as well. I think God smiles on us when we seek to have an attitude adjustment. [5]

Can you picture that love you lavish on your husband coming right back to you? When you invest in making physical intimacy sweeter in your marriage, God pours out His blessings in your life. Pam adds,

> When your relationship with your husband is the highest priority on your plate, it puts everything else in the proper perspective. The kids, the work, the house duties...it just puts everything else in the proper place when our relationship with our husband is doing well and when it's red-hot. [6]

Sweet Talk

You're in bed talking with your husband or maybe you're on a dinner date. You want to talk about your sex life, but it's awkward and you don't know how to bring it up. May I propose a simple yet highly effective strategy? Instead of starting the conversation with the word *you*, begin with the word *I*. Which conversation starter seems more welcoming?

You haven't been acting very affectionate toward me.

I haven't been acting very affectionate toward you.

What a difference those little words make! When you begin with what your husband needs to do ("You need to act more loving"), it puts him on the defense right away. But if you begin with yourself ("I would like to be more affectionate toward you during the day"), your husband will be more apt to say, "Honey, I haven't been the most affectionate spouse either." The whole tone of the conversation is now sweet, not condemning or defensive.

Meditate on verses like these when you need a little help in the sweet-talk department:

A gentle answer turns away wrath,
    but a harsh word stirs up anger.

(Proverbs 15:1)

We demolish arguments and every pretension that sets itself up against the knowledge of God, and we take captive every thought to make it obedient to Christ (2 Corinthians 10:5).

Do not let any unwholesome talk come out of your mouths, but only what is helpful for building others up according to their needs, that it may benefit those who listen (Ephesians 4:29).

His mouth is sweetness itself;
    he is altogether lovely.
This is my beloved, this is my friend,
    daughters of Jerusalem.

(Song of Songs 5:16)

If you want to enjoy more intimacy with your husband, it begins with right and true thinking about sex. Remember that intimacy usually doesn't happen by accident. It's purposeful, planned, and premeditated. That doesn't make it unromantic. On the contrary, it makes room for romance and creativity. So don't be afraid of bringing up your calendar and marking a day for lovemaking, reading up on sex, and lots of sweet talk.

Today's Picture

Think of a time when you really enjoyed making love to your husband. Where were you? What music did you listen to, if any? What was it that made it so special? How did you prepare for that time? Was it spontaneous?

Today's Prayer

Lord, help me to be creative inside and outside of the bedroom to show my husband that I love him. Keep our marriage bed undefiled. Help us both to be satisfied and excited about our love life. Draw us closer to You and to each other.

Connection and Coffee Dates

*If we walk in the light, as he is in the light, we
have fellowship with one another.*

1 JOHN 1:7

O ne thing that cracked me up about James before we got married was
how he answered the phone. Sometimes he pretended to be a pizza
place or he just cheerfully yelled out "Hello!" Or if a telemarketer called
asking for money, James would quickly turn it around and say, "Do you
have ten dollars you could lend me?" That usually ended the call abruptly.

After we were married and sharing the same phone number, these
antics became an annoyance, especially when I received a business call.
Usually, James saves his zaniness for telemarketers, but on occasion, he
goofs.

Like the time my uncle from Indonesia called. Since it was an over-
seas call, there was a slight delay, which signaled to James that this was a
telemarketer. James roared in the receiver like a king speaking to a subject,
"Speak!" Our kids started laughing, which egged him on. My uncle was
caught off guard and didn't know what to say. James then said in an over-
exaggerated accent, "Habla espanol?" ("Do you speak Spanish?"). Now
my uncle was thinking he definitely had the wrong number. James continued barking "Speak!" and joking in broken Spanish because the kids
just love all of this. Then his tone totally softened and he said, "Oh, here's
Arlene."

Now I'm mortified, thinking it's an event planner who is now *not*
going to be inviting me to be their keynote speaker. My poor uncle finally
was able to say, "Is this the right number for Arlene?" Thankfully my uncle

is a good sport and was actually relieved that he had dialed the right number. As for me, I had a new story to chuckle over and a great illustration. Sometimes you have to look at your spouse and proclaim, "Speak!"

Don't Clam Up, Communicate

When something comes between you and your man, you don't want to sweep it under the rug. You can either deal with it yourself if it's a small issue (remember from Day 18 how you can ask, *Will it matter tomorrow?*) or you need to discuss it with your husband. Ignoring problems will quickly make you unhappy and eventually bitter and angry. Instead, you want to connect positively with your spouse every day on purpose. Keep those lines of communication open. Liz Curtis Higgs has this advice about living happily with your husband:

> Here's the most important thing I've learned to have a happy husband and to be a happy wife. If something comes up between us, or I just sense Bill's unhappiness about something, the easy thing to do is to walk away and pretend I didn't see it or feel it. The better thing to do is to just say, "Honey, what's wrong?" The sooner you can air anything that's between you and get it out there, deal with it, and be done with it, the happier you'll be. We think things will go away, but they never go away. They escalate every time. So one little hurt adds to another little hurt, and by the end of the day, there's a blowup of some kind.
>
> Bill is mild-mannered, so if he really gets unhappy, I know I missed the signs twelve hours ago. When he is unhappy, something is really pressing on his heart. I think it's my job to figure out what that is, help him voice it, fix what I can, and off we go. And the air is so much clearer and it's a happy way to live. [7]

Don't Forget to Date

It's much easier to keep the lines of communication open when you are spending quality time together. James and I both work out of our home offices, so we see each other a lot throughout the day. So is it necessary for us to schedule time to see each other *again* for date night? There's actually a big difference between occupying the same space and intentionally going out to spend time together. There's something magical about getting out of your routine and looking forward to an evening out. You need to be purposeful about creating fun dates together. They can be as fancy as a five-star restaurant or as simple as a coffee date around the corner.

The next time you're out for coffee with your husband, here's something to break you out of your daily grind. Switch drinks with your spouse. You can finish it up if you like it or swap back if you need your regular brew. Talk about what it's like to live life from your spouse's perspective. Instead of "walk a mile in my shoes," think "take a sip of my coffee." What challenges is your husband facing? What made him laugh today? What's he looking forward to in the next month? Make your coffee date more meaningful by connecting with each other in a fresh way.

Kathi Lipp says you can even turn your errands into dates:

> During the busy times, dates can be running errands. The super-romantic thing we're about to do is get pet food. Before I travel, I know that's one less thing Roger has to worry about. [8]

Cindi McMenamin and her husband, Hugh, do their best to have regular date nights, although sometimes dates have to be rearranged when the unexpected comes up.

> When we have that time together at least once a week, or sometimes it's once a month, it really helps me. I'm the kind of person who needs to know there's going to be some time when we're going to be able to have that connection time. Otherwise, life seems overwhelming and I think we'll never ever connect. That connection time is like daily maintenance on the car. Keep everything in check so you don't have a breakdown.
>
> Having traditions helps. Hugh loves to get ice cream after a meal. Do you know what I will look like if I have ice cream after every single meal? But this is what makes him happy, and I'm going to do it. And I just have to hit the exercise class a little harder. [9]

Does your husband still make you laugh? I like this short conversation between two friends:

> "Bill's wife always laughs at his jokes."
>
> "They must be pretty clever."
>
> "No—she is." [10]

Don't let your husband's jokes or your date nights grow stale. Be a wise and happy wife who is purposeful about dating and making daily connections. If need be, you can always try James's tactic by belting out "Speak!" if you're having a hard time getting the conversation going.

Today's Picture

You're a fly on the wall, watching you and your husband on a date when you were engaged. See how you laugh at his jokes, hold hands, and cuddle often? You're affectionate, playful, and happy.

Today's Prayer

Lord, thank You that my husband is not only my partner in marriage, he's my best friend and closest companion. Help me to be a fun, affectionate companion to him today. Bring us back to our first love, when we longed to be together and enjoyed just being in each other's company. Help us to connect in a meaningful way every day in our marriage. Deliver us from evil and let Your will be done in us. We are forever Yours.

Death by Neglect

Go to the ant...
consider its ways and be wise!
PROVERBS 6:6

James has some great college buddies who now live all across the United States. Every few years, just James and the boys get together for a weekend reunion. They've watched a baseball game at Wrigley Field, skied in Canada, and spotted whales in the San Juan Islands. I actually love when James goes away with the guys for a few days because when he comes back, he's in full "I love my wife" mode. He's missed me. He's waxed nostalgic with his friends and can see how far we've come as a couple. He's ready to kiss, cuddle, and talk sweetly to me. I'm a happy wife, basking in all the attention!

There are times in marriage when appreciation is in full bloom. Maybe your husband returns from a long business trip and you really missed him. Or you've spent time with a friend going through a divorce and you realize how blessed you really are. Yet the opposite reality is true too. You go through days, maybe even months, when you take your spouse for granted (and vice versa). If you're not purposeful to stoke the fire of your relationship, you may experience a slow death by neglect without even realizing it.

The Way of the Ant

Perhaps you sometimes feel as if your marriage is a heavy burden and just plain hard work. Take a deep breath and relax. Today, all you have to do is consider the habits of a tiny ant. The ants mentioned in Proverbs are most likely harvester ants that live in underground nests. They are most active during the summer, collecting large amounts of grain from the fields, threshing floors, and barns. Ants don't hibernate. In the winter, they mate, lay their eggs, and care for their young with provisions saved up from the summer.

Maybe you can relate to these little ants because you've felt as if you were living underground, invisible to the outside world and even to your husband. Plus there are no seasons to "clock out" as a wife, no such thing as hibernation. Here's how the book of Proverbs praises the ant:

> Go to the ant, you sluggard
> consider its ways and be wise!
> It has no commander,
> no overseer or ruler,
> yet it stores its provisions in summer
> and gathers its food at harvest.
> (Proverbs 6:6-8)

> Ants are creatures of little strength,
> yet they store up their food in the summer.
> (Proverbs 30:25)

These minute insects are applauded because of their planning and industrious nature. They may be small in strength, but they are exceedingly wise in preparing for the future. During seasons of plenty, they store up. When the food supply dries up, they are well-stocked with everything they need because they've planned for the lean times.

The wise and happy wife does the same thing. You plan for times of plenty and times of need in your marriage. You work to gather things that nurture your marriage and you're not caught off guard when winter comes. You store up shared happy memories, hugs, kisses, and kind words. You're not lazy about your marriage. On the contrary, you're industrious because you know food for your marriage won't automatically appear on your doorstep. If you're neglectful during the good times, you won't have anything to draw from when the tough times come.

Sharon Jaynes puts it this way:

> If you know a hurricane is coming, you prepare for that hurricane. You store up water, you store up food. You make sure you

are ready for a storm. Well, you never know when a hurricane is going to hit your marriage, so you have to prepare before it hits. It's very important to read books, to grow spiritually together, and to be purposeful to read God's Word together. Put the principles into practice and make sure you are growing in the Lord together before the hurricane. [11]

Doing Dishes

Some days you're facing a hurricane. Other days you're simply trying to get through your routine. Small things have to be done every day, no matter how mundane. Brushing your teeth, walking the dog, and checking email come to mind. And what about those pesky dishes? It turns out that household chores are becoming more of a hotbed issue for married couples. According to a Pew Research Center survey, "sharing household chores" now ranks third in a list of items that make a successful marriage (behind faithfulness and a happy sexual relationship). In the poll, 62 percent of adults said that sharing household chores is very important in a happy marriage. [12]

Household chores include things like meal preparation, cleaning, outdoor work, childcare, organization, and paying bills. Yikes, I didn't mean to inject stress into today's reading! How do you and your husband divide labor in the home? Although this can be a tense conversation, it should not be ignored or neglected. If one partner thinks he or she has an unfair share of work, that opens the door for resentment.

If you tackle your household responsibilities on purpose, assigning jobs to the best-suited person and treating every day as a team sport, you will find joy even in those dirty dishes. James has automated most of our bill paying. I cook (well, mostly assemble) dinner on typical days. James and I both do dishes. I shop for the kids, and he shops for anything with a plug or a battery.

Pay Attention to the Little Things

Peggy Noonan was a speechwriter for Ronald Reagan. When people would ask her what President Reagan was like, she would often share "the bathroom story":

> A few days after he'd been shot, when he could get out of bed, he wasn't feeling well one night and went to the bathroom

connected to his room. He slapped water on his face, and water slopped out of the sink. He got some paper towels and got on the floor to clean it up. And an aide came in and said, "Mr. President, what are you doing? We have people for that." And Reagan said oh, no, he was just cleaning up his mess, he didn't want a nurse to have to do it. [13]

President Reagan not only acted with great character in moments of crisis or war, he acted with character in the tiny things, even stooping to clean up water he had spilled in a hospital bathroom.

May we act in this way, not neglecting our responsibilities as a wife, no matter how mundane or insignificant they may seem. Don't wait until your spouse goes out of town before you appreciate his presence in your life and lavish him with love. Don't let the household chores get you down or discouraged. Remember the diligence of the ant?

Today's Picture

Picture a framed photograph of you and your groom on your wedding day. It's been a while since you handled it, so it's covered with a thick layer of dust. You take out a rag and shine it up. There. That's better. What's one small action you can do today to "dust off" your marriage?

Today's Prayer

Lord, I know You care about how I handle the small and big issues of my life. Help me to learn from the ant to be diligent and hard working. I want to be industrious in my marriage. Please forgive me for being neglectful of my spouse and even of myself. When the storms come to my home, I want to be ready. Transform me into an attentive spouse who cares about building a marriage that will stand the test of time.

I'm Bored

*She watches over the affairs of her household
and does not eat the bread of idleness.*

PROVERBS 31:27

M y son Ethan came home from elementary school, long-faced, drag-
ging his heels. Since he wasn't his usual peppy self, I asked, "How
was school?"

"Okay," he replied in a monotone voice. "But I didn't learn anything
new. It was boring, boring, boring."

At bedtime, we talked more about his blasé day.

"I've done everything I like at recess. There's nothing new to try. I just
walked around. I played a little bit of dodgeball. I talked to a few friends.
That was it. It was so boring."

Inside, I was smiling and thinking, *If my son thinks recess, dodgeball,
and talking to friends is boring, wait until he gets to college lectures, paying
bills, and working his first job!* I told him that adults felt bored too, and that
boredom was just a part of life. Not every day is Disneyland, new concepts,
and fancy foods. I also added, in mom-like fashion, "If you are bored, it's
up to you to find something interesting to do."

Just like Ethan, we as wives can say, "I'm bored." We can whine, complain, and fuss about the dull routine of married life, doing the same thing
every day and going apparently nowhere. We're running in circles with
the same man, eating at the same restaurants, fighting over the same issues.
We're trapped, not in a bad marriage but in boredom.

It's as Easy as E, F, G

You know the saying "It's as easy as A, B, C"? Well, a bored wife can get herself into trouble as easy as E, F, G.

Escape—If you're not satisfied with your everyday life, why not escape? Some women escape by shopping. You can shop in a store or just order things online in the comfort of your home. With a click of the mouse, your boring life can be transformed by a new purse, pair of shoes, or jacket. Or you can escape into the kitchen for some cookies, ice cream, chips, or cake. Too bad celery doesn't provide this same escape!

Fantasy—Have you noticed that steamy romance novels geared for women are becoming more popular? Men aren't the only ones interested in fantasy in the bedroom. If a bored wife decides to spice things up with some soft porn, that fantasy life can lead to some real-life problems with her real-life husband. The only person you want to be fantasizing about is your man.

Gossip—If you don't have a juicy life, why not make up one and talk about it? Or listen to the exciting tales of a friend's life? As someone said in *Good Housekeeping* years ago, "It isn't the people who tell all they know that cause most of the trouble in this world, it's the ones who tell more." [14]

Thankfully, there's a way to avoid the traps of escaping to bad habits, fantasizing about someone who's not our husband, and gossiping. When you are purposeful as a wife, with goals and dreams for your marriage, you will be too busy and focused to get sidetracked for long.

Boredom Is a Choice

Pam Farrel, who is definitely not a bored wife, says that boredom is a choice:

> We can choose to allow God to make us into amazing women regardless of the people around us and their choices. That's the best way to not be bored. Say I want to be the best me I can be. God doesn't say, "I'm going to let you be the best you only if your husband cooperates," or "I'm going to let you be the best you only if your husband makes so much money." No, He will work around circumstances and through circumstances to help us become the very best us.
>
> I encourage women to look for God's personal Post-it notes of

goodness. My friend calls it kisses from heaven. If we look for those things, we start seeing our lives differently, more from God's perspective. It could be a Facebook post, a verse during quiet times, or a note from a friend. They are little things that add up in a big way. [15]

Expect God to speak to you and look around for ways to join in God's work. The virtuous wife described in Proverbs 31 hates to sit still and do nothing. She does not eat the bread of idleness. She knows that when we're bored and lack direction, it's easy to waste time on frivolous things that can tear down our house. She's careful to fill her time with service to her family and community.

Carol Kent and her husband, Gene, look for people in their circle of friends who need help worse than they do. Carol says,

> We are very intentional about doing one tangible act of kindness for that person because that is one way we can touch their lives, with just a sparkle of joy and encouragement in the middle of their difficult time. It might be groceries for a single mom or reaching out to people with incarcerated loved ones. [16]

When you set your sights on serving others, you will never be bored or lonely. Billy Graham said it so well, "Only those who want everything done for them are bored." [17]

Stay Interesting

What Marjorie Blanchard says about fighting monotony in marriage is extremely wise:

> I think women and men need to stay interesting to themselves. They need to pursue their own interests and also to look carefully for something they can share with their spouse. I think men love to have a pal, and if you can find some things that you both like doing, I think that's very important in a marriage. The other thing that's very important is for men and women to develop their own interests. Ask yourself, *What's new on my resume in the last three years?* [18]

If you have been feeling bored in your marriage, what are a few things *you* could do to change that? Remember, you're not going to wait around for your husband to fix things for you. You are going to be proactive by:

- Planning a date to a new restaurant
- Trying a new activity together, such as kayaking, dancing, photography, or running
- Spending time doing something you really love
- Finding somewhere to volunteer that you both enjoy
- Having a candlelight dinner at home
- Journaling about ten things you are thankful for in your marriage
- You fill in the blank: _____

You're now motivated to take the words "I'm bored" out of your vocabulary. Most pleasant memories don't just happen; they must be arranged in advance. In the same way you planned a surprise birthday party for a family member or friend, you've got to plan to make happy memories with your husband.

Don't check out of your marriage emotionally, physically, or spiritually when boredom hits. Realize that the blahs come to everyone. Those who have successful marriages learn how to keep boredom at bay by constantly growing. Be intentional about keeping your marriage interesting and fun. Avoid uttering the words "I'm bored" and instead say, "I think we should try…"

Today's Picture

What are three activities you are currently not doing that you and your husband would enjoy?

1.

2.

3.

Today's Prayer

Lord, Your Word says in Proverbs 4:23 to guard my heart more than anything else, because the source of my life flows from it. Keep my heart pure from destructive things like gossip and ungodly fantasies. Help me to turn my boredom into positive actions that will cause me to grow in my spirit, mind, and heart. Give me strength to run the race of my life with endurance with my eye on the prize.

Beyond These Walls

The one who lives with integrity is righteous;
his children who come after him will be happy.
Proverbs 20:7 (hcsb)

I grew up with a happy mom. She laughs easily, smiles broadly at everyone she meets, and even jumps up and down if she hasn't seen you for a while. My school friends would ask me, "Is your mom always this happy?" She and my father were a great example of *happily ever after* as I grew up.

But what if you never had a model of what a happy wife should act like? Maybe your parents divorced when you were young or they fought a lot. Sharon Jaynes can relate. She grew up in a beautiful neighborhood lined with tall pine trees. By outward appearances, she lived in a normal, happy American family. Her father was a successful businessman who traveled much of the time. Sadly, his success in business didn't translate to his home life. He drank heavily, terrorized the home, and beat his wife.

Changing the Family Tree

Sharon became a Christian when she was a teenager, and six years later, her parents came to know Jesus and their lives were forever changed for the better. But it was too late for Sharon to experience a do-over as a child in a healthier home. So when she got married in her twenties, she needed guidance.

> I did not have a role model in my mother to know what a happy wife should be like. But I had others to look up to, including the woman who led me to the Lord. What drew me to their house and what drew me to her was her joy. I would watch her walking

through her house singing praise songs as she cleaned. She and her husband had pet names for each other. They loved each other so much, and that really drew me to their home. And it made me want to know about Jesus.

Sharon and her husband watched Christian families around them and emulated what they saw. They spent time in God's Word and time with other Christian couples.

I determined that when I got married I was going to do everything within my power to have a good marriage and be a happy wife. But I learned very quickly that it was not in my own power to do that. I knew the only way I could be a happy wife and we could have a good happy marriage was to have our marriage centered on Jesus Christ. And that's what we did from the very beginning. God taught me through His Word. We made sure that we had relationships with mature Christian couples and we learned from them. If we had a question or problem, we would go to them. We made sure that in our marriage, nothing would sit and simmer.

After being married a few years, Sharon had their first child. One of their goals was to show their son Steven what a good marriage looks like. Sharon was able to give her child a precious gift that she did not have when she was growing up.

I did purpose to have a happy home. People think it's going to happen automatically. They usually have a wakeup call when they realize that automatic doesn't work! So we were very purposeful in what we did. That was true in our marriage and that was true in our parenting as well.

Here we've been married more than thirty-two years, and we are still learning and growing. God uses marriage probably more than any other relationship on earth to refine us, change us, grow us, and mature us to be the men and women He intended us to be.[19]

Making New Rules

Take a moment to answer this basic yet often ignored question: What do you want in *your* marriage? Marjorie Blanchard offers this perspective to help you process that question for yourself:

> It takes a certain amount of introspection to understand what you want. I think it's a lot easier for people to tell you what they *don't* want than to tell you what they *do* want. If you can figure out what you want and talk with your spouse about it, you are way down the road. Very often people just react to what they don't like, but they never get to that next stage, which is, "What do I value? What do I want? What is the standard that I want to hold for myself?" [20]

Years ago, when Marjorie was working hard at her doctorate and Ken was busy promoting his leadership books, Marjorie realized they needed to establish some new rules. She figured out that the one thing that really bothered her was that Ken was away on most weekends, leaving her alone with their two children, who were nine and eleven. They made a new rule to be together on most weekends, and that helped them through a busy and stressful time that could have potentially driven them apart.

In the past five years, their new rule has been to have a daily time of ten to fifteen minutes to pray and read together. Ken loves to read a daily devotional out loud to Marjorie, and it gives them a special time to connect spiritually each day.

What are the new rules you would like to see in your marriage? Begin with a bit of introspection. *What do you want in your marriage?* When you get ahold of that answer, you can work with your husband to build that happy home together. The impact of your joy and satisfaction will resonate far beyond four walls.

Today's Picture

Think of your home as a hub where many people come to be nourished. It's primarily a place for refreshment for you and your husband. If you have kids, they come into your home to find a place of security. Your friends come over to experience a place of peace and joy. Your home is a light in your neighborhood, and your marriage serves as a shining example of God's love.

Today's Prayer

Lord, You are the light of the world. Shine Your light into my marriage and show me what is most important for me to focus on right now. Regardless of my past, I give You my future and dedicate my home for Your glory. I will not be held back by past mistakes and regrets. I will look to You for new purpose and strength. May others look at my marriage and see You working in us and through us.

Day 25

Most Valuable Prayers

The prayer of a righteous [wife] is powerful and effective.

JAMES 5:16

You've probably prayed these words before, *Dear Lord, bless my husband.* I certainly have said these words year after year at bedtime or whenever James crosses my mind. While this is good, I wonder if there's a more purposeful and powerful way to pray for my husband. Prayer can be intimidating to many of us. What if we don't say the right words? Does God really work through our prayers? When are you supposed to fit in the time to pray anyway?

Prayer can seem like a sacred, secret activity reserved for specially gifted intercessors or grandmas with gobs of time on their hands. But that is a terrible misconception. A meaningful prayer life is available to every age group and every wife, so that includes you.

The Positive Side of Desperation

When you are busy (and who isn't?), you must be purposeful about prayer or it just doesn't happen. Kathi Lipp has some encouraging words about getting started:

> I have to do the kindergarten version of prayer. I need to give myself reminders, so I put Post-it notes around me. When Roger is in crisis, it's easy to know specifically how to pray for him. It's when he's not in crisis that I have to be diligent and say, *You know what, he needs my prayers whether I think he needs them or not.* He's a different guy when I'm praying for him. He walks more

confidently. He is bolder at work when he needs to be. He's more patient. It's not a coincidence. Often he will say, "I know you're praying for me. I knew you had my back." It makes me feel like I can be that supportive wife that I really desire to be. [21]

I have a feeling you want to be that prayerful, supportive wife that makes your husband stand taller and live bolder. When I interviewed John Fuller for *31 Days to a Happy Husband,* he talked about the strength he received from knowing his wife, Dena, was praying for him. John and Dena have six kids and their youngest has autism. I asked Dena how she found the time to pray in the midst of a hectic family schedule. She told me the quick answer was "desperation!"

When you're going through difficult times, you quickly realize you can't do everything in your own power. Dena sees throughout Scripture that suffering is a part of life. There is something inherent about problems and crises that brings us to our knees. Dena shares,

> I sometimes wonder what kind of Christian I would be if hardship and trials did not come into my home. By nature as human beings, we cruise when things go along well. I wish that were not so. I do think that suffering of any kind will help us become more fervent in prayer. A lot of my prayers are just tears before God. I have begged with God, I've bargained with God, I've pleaded with God, you name it. I don't think there's this correct way to pray and that I have to have all the words right. Pouring my heart out before God is a form of prayer. I often ask God to show me how to pray. *Could You give me clarity, Lord, so I can pray in line with Your will and not just what I want?*

Dena enjoys reading books on prayer to encourage her to grow in this essential area as a wife. Her prayers for John have helped her have a more gracious and warm attitude toward him.

> When you begin to pray for someone, you start to see the struggles they are going through and how difficult that must be. And then all of a sudden you feel more compassionate instead of seeing what you wished was changed. *I wish he wouldn't travel so much* or *I wish he could get home earlier.* You start to see things from his point of view.

John just traveled yesterday and he was exhausted. This was not a pleasure trip for him. I think praying for him helps me ask God, *What would You have me pray for him?* I see some areas where I think he really needs God, but I might be missing the boat. He might have something else entirely different that he needs me to be praying for.

Years ago, when John was offered the position of cohost for the national radio program *Focus on the Family*, Dena felt fear. A more private person, she had pictured a more anonymous life of service for their family.

We had quite a lot of talks and walks and prayer. In that season together praying for the decision, God gave me an assurance that this was not about John and it wasn't about me. It was about God's purposes. The Lord said, *You have to put this in My hands. That's not a life of faith to pull back in fear.* That was a time when praying for the decision really melded John and me with each other and with God. [22]

John's trusted voice has been heard on the radio around the world because of what was confirmed in Dena's heart through prayer. When you don't know what to do at the fork in the road, pray. And don't forget when all is calm and bright, that's the ideal time to pray too.

Not Talent But Tenacity

I don't know much about sports, but I do know that MVP stands for Most Valuable Player. MVPs don't only have natural talent; they are driven, patient, disciplined, and tenacious. May I give you a new title to wear proudly? You are the MVP—Most Valuable Prayer—in your marriage (so is your husband, but this is a book for us wives). If you want to bring your family team to victory, you will accomplish the greatest gains through prayer.

Stormie Omartian, author of *The Power of a Praying Wife*, says there's so much at stake if we *don't* pray.

Can you imagine praying for the right side of your body and not the left? If the right side is not sustained and protected and it falls, it's going to bring down the left side with it. The same is true of you and your husband. If you pray for yourself and not him, you will never find the blessings and fulfillment you want. What happens to him happens to you and you can't get around it. [23]

The happy wife prays for her husband and lives in the confidence that God has it all under control. You don't need talent to pray. You simply need tenacity. Don't give up. Use the Word of God and like the psalmist cry,

> I lift up my eyes to the mountains—
> where does my help come from?
> My help comes from the LORD,
> the Maker of heaven and earth.
>
> (Psalm 121:1-2)

Pick up the help line often because God is always waiting for your call.

Today's Picture

Imagine you are receiving a trophy. The audience is clapping loudly for you. Your husband is seated in the front row, cheering like crazy. Engraved on the gold placard, it reads MVP: Most Valuable Prayer. It becomes one of your most prized possessions.

Today's Prayer

Lord, I don't want to trust in people or technology to fix my problems. I want to run to You. Like the disciples I cry out, "Lord, teach me to pray." I want to be a prayer warrior for my husband, seeking Your protection, favor, and blessing in his life. I don't want to pray only when I need something. I want to praise You daily and pray continually with thanksgiving and faith. Help my unbelief. May my prayers be in line with Your will. Make them powerful and effective in the name of Jesus, amen.

Focus 5

HOPEFUL

ADAPTABLE

POSITIVE

PURPOSEFUL

Becoming YIELDED

Day 26

Who's in Control?

*"You will desire to control your husband,
but he will rule over you."*

Genesis 3:16 (nlt)

A few years ago, my family was vacationing on Kona, the big island of Hawaii. Sounds idyllic right? Yet on day three of the vacation, the island's active volcano wasn't the only thing getting ready to blow. For the first two days, we had done many activities that James enjoys. With him in mind, I had planned hikes off the beaten path (translation: no restroom for miles), packed picnics and lots of snacks for the kids. Here's a page from my vacation diary as I stewed in my thoughts:

> Why doesn't he ask me what *I* want to do? I wouldn't mind going to the pool for two hours and then walking through the touristy shops at Kailua-Kona. How come I always plan the vacation with *him* in mind? Why doesn't he ask me what I want to do? What I really want is regular access to a bathroom!

I didn't want to be mad at James during our vacation. I tried to see things from his perspective. He wasn't trying to be mean and he hadn't really done anything wrong. He just wanted to have a good time on his vacation, and what's wrong with that? The kids and I do enjoy hiking; I just like the touristy things more than James does.

I decided to ask God to show me what to do. I would respect James's desires in planning the itinerary, and I hoped he would show me love by asking what I would prefer to do. I asked the Lord to work in the next twenty-four hours, and then I thought if nothing happened, I would bring it up to James.

We were sharing a vacation rental with my parents, and at the very next meal my mom was the chosen spokesperson. She gave poor James a mini-lecture about how we should be safer with all of the kids and that he should ask me what I wanted to do. I hadn't breathed a word to her about any of this. She talked to him so much that I didn't feel the need to add one word. God had answered my prayer at the first opportunity, and hours later, James asked if I wanted to stop at the coffee farm for a latte. He doesn't even drink coffee. There we were, relaxed and happy, caffeinated and near a restroom. Now this was more like vacation!

I learned something valuable on that big island. I discovered that I don't have to take matters into my own hands and insist on my rights. When I'm not happy with a decision, I should not prepare my case with the force of a district attorney. The most effective thing to do is to pray and ask God to be my advocate before speaking out. In day-to-day life, and even on vacation, we have to work together with our spouse, compromising and doing the dance of give and take. The danger comes when we insist on taking the wheel.

Deadlock in Wedlock

The idea of yielding to your husband may be the hardest principle in this book for you to swallow. Perhaps that's why it's the last letter to cover:

H = Hopeful
A = Adaptable
P = Positive
P = Purposeful
Y = Yielded

There are many misunderstandings today about submission, control, and leadership within a marriage. The husband who is overly authoritative and emotionally abusive can manipulate his wife to her destruction, all in the name of male leadership. I hope you do not fall into this category and that your husband does not hold you under his thumb. I hope you have a voice in your marriage. If you are married to a good and decent man, yielding to his leadership in the home is a wise decision. If you're not too comfortable with that, take it up with Eve.

After Adam and Eve sinned in the garden, God described for Eve one of the consequences of their disobedience:

> "I will sharpen the pain of your pregnancy,
> and in pain you will give birth.
> And you will desire to control your husband,
> but he will rule over you."
>
> (Genesis 3:16 NLT)

Listen to this helpful explanation of this verse by Karen Ehman, author of *Let. It. Go.*:

> In the original Hebrew, the phrase that is translated, "Your desire shall be for your husband" actually means that a woman's desire would be for her husband's *position*. Meaning, he would be the pants wearer in the family, but she would want to wiggle her sweet little self into them instead and leave him holding a fig leaf...As a woman you'll desire to be the boss, but your husband has already been assigned that job description. Bummer.[1]

You don't have to look far in popular culture, or even within the walls of your own home, to see this tug-of-war played out between a husband and wife. These quotes are funny because we've all been there at one time:

- "My wife and I have an agreement—I don't try to run her life and I don't try to run mine."

- "Compromise in marriage is an amiable arrangement between husband and wife whereby they agree to let her have her own way."[2]

Yet the Bible tells us there is a divine order of creation: "But I want you to realize that the head of every man is Christ, and the head of the woman is man, and the head of Christ is God" (1 Corinthians 11:3).

In other words, every man is responsible to Christ, a woman is responsible to her husband, and Christ is responsible to God. If Christ was humble enough to submit to the authority of His Father's will (see Matthew 26:39), certainly we as humans are not above submission. As you think about what God's Word says about yielding to others (including your husband) and esteeming others as better than yourself, you will be changed and softened for the better. Liz Curtis Higgs says,

> I think being in God's Word recreates us at a cellular level. I really do. I think we are made new in our very demeanor, in our temperament, and how we handle everything. I think a husband notices that. Your gentleness, your patience, whatever it was that you didn't have much of, as you grow more in those areas it will stand out to him. And you'll have a relationship with God that's so sweet.
>
> Isaiah 54:5 says, "For your Maker is your husband—the LORD Almighty is his name." When we really make God our husband— absolutely the one we are most in love with, beholden to, and obedient to—there's not a man alive who wouldn't want that woman for a wife. She's going to be sweeter, she's going to be more loving, and she's going to be stronger too. It isn't a matter of becoming a doormat—no way! A woman who knows she is loved by God and is focused on Him is a powerful and strong woman for all the right reasons. The bottom line is a happy wife is a woman who is happy with her Lord. [3]

There's Always the U-Turn

A few years ago, I got a speeding ticket on my way home from Costco. I remember telling the police officer that I was very sorry, but I was speeding because my little girl needed her nap and my little boy said he had to go to the bathroom. I still got the ticket. I decided to attend traffic school to reduce my fine, and at the end of my long day in class, we played *Jeopardy* to review. One of the questions was, "What's it called when you're driving down the street and you turn to go in the opposite direction?" Can you believe the woman sitting in front of me passed on that question? I saved my team with the brilliant answer, "U-turn."

If you've been fighting for control in your marriage and you've been heading in the wrong direction, today is a great day to make a U-turn. After all, it might just save your husband-and-wife team.

Today's Picture

Imagine you are driving down a highway labeled "My Life." There's a fork in the road. One direction has a sign that says "I stay in control." The other direction says "I give control to God." Which path do you choose and why?

Today's Prayer

Lord, create in me a clean heart and renew a right spirit in me. I yield to Your Holy Spirit today. Have Your way in my life. Help me to give control of my life over to You. I can't see the future as You can. I trust in Your judgment and commit my plans into Your care.

Day 27

Father Does Know Best

Therefore the LORD is waiting to show you mercy,
and is rising up to show you compassion,
for the LORD is a just God.
all who wait patiently for Him are happy.

ISAIAH 30:18 (HCSB)

This morning James put a pot of oatmeal on the stove and set the timer for six minutes. He told Ethan to turn off the stove when the timer beeped. I walked in the kitchen as it was beeping. Obediently, Ethan turned off the heat, but I could see the oatmeal needed some more fire. But I figured, *James said to turn it off. We'll just do that and see what happens.* After all, last week I had ruined the oatmeal.

A few minutes later, James walked in the kitchen and said to me, "Why did you turn the oatmeal off? Can't you see it needs to cook more?"

I overrode my common sense about the oatmeal, figuring I could blame James since he was the one who said to turn it off when the timer beeped. Sometimes there's a tension between obeying our husband's leadership and using common sense, isn't there? And there's also the hierarchy of listening to God's voice above all. Cindi McMenamin sheds light on this important balance:

> Because I married a pastor and a wonderful man, it was very easy to put him in the place of God and not realize it in my life. Hugh can't possible meet all my needs. He can't be the one who can fulfill me and give me my sense of purpose. He can't meet every one of my emotional needs. I had to go to God first. I had to yield

to God and see Him as my spiritual husband. My primary fulfillment and sustenance comes from the Lord. That took a huge
weight off Hugh, and it also made me a happy wife. Suddenly
I wasn't putting that burden on my husband and I wasn't that
unfulfilled woman. [4]

Only God Can Carry You

Even more important than yielding to your husband is yielding to
God. Are you able to submit yourself to God's will even when His plan
seems to be colliding with your own? Jesus Himself had to pray in the garden of Gethsemane, "My Father! If it is possible, let this cup of suffering be
taken away from me. Yet I want your will to be done, not mine" (Matthew
26:39 NLT). Jesus yielded to His Father's will even though it brought pain.

If you are a living, breathing human being, you have experienced suffering. It is an inevitable part of life. My darkest time came when I was
twenty weeks pregnant with our second child. It was supposed to be a season of joy and anticipation. It was the day before Thanksgiving, and my
in-laws had traveled across the country to celebrate with us. We were all
crammed in an examination room, anxious to find out from the ultrasound if I was having a boy or a girl. The technician was strangely quiet
and informed us at the end of the appointment that we were having a girl.
We were ecstatic!

But our joy was short-lived. Later that day the telephone rang, and it
was my doctor. "Arlene, I hate to tell you this, but your baby has serious
chromosomal defects and she isn't going to make it. She will probably die
in the womb in the next few days. I'd really like you to go to the specialist
today for a detailed ultrasound so you don't have to go through the entire
Thanksgiving weekend not knowing."

Hours later, the specialist confirmed that our baby's heart would stop
beating within days, maybe one to two weeks at most. That Thanksgiving
was the hardest one of our lives. I was experiencing a real-life practicum to
see if I really could give thanks in all circumstances. I didn't have to thank
God *for* a sick baby, but I could thank Him that He was walking with me.

No matter what I did physically, I could not change the outcome of
my baby's health. Eating vegetables, getting extra sleep, or going for a
walk would not help my baby. I could do nothing to control what was

happening in my womb. Don't we as women long for that control? And when we can't control our circumstances, we worry. But worry doesn't help either. It was *trust* that was going to get me through.

> Trust in the LORD with all your heart
> and lean not on your own understanding.
>
> (Proverbs 3:5)

Every week, I drove to the doctor's office, crying out to God in the car. I prayed that God would heal my baby, take her home to heaven, or give us grace to care for a special-needs child. Week after week, that little baby's heart kept beating. Week after week, I prayed, *Your kingdom come, Your will be done.*

I received the bad news the day before Thanksgiving, and on Christmas Day, I was still pregnant. I was thankful our baby was still with us for Christmas, but before the New Year came, that little girl slipped from my womb into eternity. I discovered in those hard days that when you live with your hand open to God instead of balled up in an angry fist, it's much easier to find healing. I reached out to God in brokenness and asked Him to take my hand and lead me out of that dark valley—and He did.

We named our baby Angel Rose and had a memorial service for her at the beach to say good-bye. On her due date, April 7, I took a pregnancy test and it was positive! One Christmas, we were saying good-bye to Angel Rose. The very next Christmas, we were holding a healthy baby girl in our arms named Noelle Joy.

I couldn't have engineered that story and happy ending. And I wouldn't trade the lessons I learned about letting go of control and letting God lead the way.

> When I let go of control
> Allowing you to take the lead
> I find rest for my weary soul
>
> When I let go of control
> Yielding to your will and ways
> I find peace about my every need
>
> When I let go of control
> Putting your word to the test
> I finally discover Father does know best

No Longer the Queen of Worry

When you become friends with the idea that God is in control and Father really does know best, it allows you to free yourself of worry. My friend Chris Montgomery is a director of children's ministries at a church. She blogged about being the queen of worry.

> The antidote to worry is to pray with thanksgiving (Philippians 4:6-7). Granted, that doesn't come easy to me. Worry? I've had lots of experience and I'm pretty good at it. Yet the illusion of control that it brings is just that, an illusion.
>
> I have this mental picture that I combine with actual physical movement. I cup my hands, and picture them full of all those chaotic, unsettling emotions. Raising them to the Lord as an offering, I turn my hands upside down and consciously release all the stress and worry to Him. Finally, I raise my hands to Him, again cupping them, but this time it is so He can fill them with what He has for me instead.
>
> Sweet tendrils of peace slowly wrap themselves around my anxious spirit. I give up worry and gain trust. I trade my anxiousness for His peace. It pleases God and allows me to sleep at night. Praise God, the queen has been dethroned. [5]

Let Father God take control of your life. There's no need for you to worry and work night and day to engineer your life. Let go—God's got you covered.

Today's Picture

Cup your hands and picture them full of your worries and unsettling emotions. Raise them up to God as an offering, and then drop all those concerns at His feet. Cup your hands once again and ask God to fill you with His peace and wisdom.

Today's Prayer

Lord, I give You my anxiety and concerns. Your Word says to cast my cares on You because You care for me. Thank You for loving me and for knowing what I need even before I know myself. I trust in Your ways even when I don't understand what is happening around me. I choose to place my hope in You. You are never changing and always able to meet every one of my needs and much more. Dear Father, take control of my life.

Stepping Up and Stepping Down

*"Be strong and courageous, because you will
lead these people to inherit the land
I swore to their ancestors to give them."*

Joshua 1:6

Consider the mass appeal of blockbusters like *Gladiator* and *Braveheart*. Those movies are centered on men of great courage who stepped up when everyone else backed down. As wives, don't we long for a strong man like that to rescue and protect us when necessary? But maybe your superhero looks more like a couch potato. Guess what? You can be instrumental in his transformation.

If your husband feels usurped by your control in the home, after a while he will stop trying to lead. He will defer the big and small decisions to you. Certainly there is give and take in marriage. You are not to be a silent partner while he calls all the shots. But when your husband thinks you wear the pants in the family, it's demoralizing to him. Your dissatisfaction with his leadership will lead to passivity. His passivity will lead to more of your dissatisfaction. And that unhealthy cycle spins around and around.

The modern woman wishes her man would step up to the plate and take responsibility. But when he does step up, he's often met with criticism instead of praise. When we tell our husbands to step up, we must also be prepared to step down and make room for his leadership.

The Best Way

John Wooden, the former coach of the record-setting UCLA basketball team, won ten national championships in twelve years. Yet with all of his success on the court, he believed he had an even more successful marriage. In his book *Wooden: A Lifetime of Observations and Reflections On and Off the Court,* he wrote:

> Did your marriage start from love? Of course it did. So, look back. Were you more considerate then? Have you lost that for some reason? Marriage requires that each partner listen to the other side. It's like what I say about leadership: "You must be interested in finding the best way, not in having your own way." The same is true in marriage. Don't be stubborn and insist on having your own way. Look to find a way that works for both of you. [6]

You must be interested in finding the best way. Think of your relationship with your husband. Do you press for your way or for the mutually best way? Do you back up his decisions and allow him to lead in the home? My kids know if they ask me for ice cream and I say yes, but then it comes out that James had already said no, there's no discussion. I will say, "I didn't know that Daddy said no. You know that Daddy makes the final decision." Sometimes I disagree with his decision, but that is secondary to my commitment to honor him in our home.

Like the time he forced me to step up even when I had a bum ankle. I was recovering from a sprained ankle, so I couldn't do any exercises that put pressure on my ankle. A perfect time for a vacation from the gym, right? Not so according to my personal coach, James. He declared that swimming would be perfect for me. He said he would watch the kids so I could go swim at the gym.

But I didn't *want* to go swimming. I'm not a good swimmer (think doggie paddle). I wear contact lenses and don't like getting under the water. But without my contacts, I'm as blind as a non-swimming bat. I had watched the people in the pool and they certainly didn't swim like me. As James prodded me to get my bathing suit and get going, I said some words to him that would not fit my "happy wife" profile. I moaned all the way to the car, dragged myself into that locker room, and into the foreign land of the swimming pool.

At first the water was cold. I was miserable and embarrassed. But after a lap or two (and the comfort of someone a few lanes down who looked more foolish than I did), I began to enjoy myself. When it was all said and done, I was happy for the exercise. Yielding to James had been painful at the time, but the end result was very positive. Swimming became my exercise staple while my ankle healed.

Yielding to your husband can feel like stepping into a cold pool. *Should I really be doing this? Hmm, this feels uncomfortable. Maybe I should get out.* But, my friend, if you stick with it, you'll be in perfect stroke with your husband in just a few laps.

Dig for Courage

In his book *Stepping Up: A Call to Courageous Manhood,* Dennis Rainey writes,

> I believe there's something in the chest of a man that responds in a unique way to stories of courage. There's a piece of every man's heart that longs to be courageous, to be bold and gutsy and etch a masculine mark of bravery on the human landscape...
>
> Real courage is doing your duty under fire. And we all face situations throughout our lives that require that type of courage. Valor at home, protecting our wives and children. Moral courage in the marketplace. Becoming the men God created us to be, despite whatever pressures we face in the world. [7]

Your husband wants to rise up to be the hero in your life. You're the only one who can allow him the privilege of protecting and guiding you. If your home is the stage on which real life is played out, your husband doesn't want to fight you for the leading role. But if you step down, you will give him the courage to step up. Many men are afraid to step up and lead because they don't know if they will fail or succeed. You can give him the assurance that you would rather have him try and fail than to be a passive member of the family.

Perhaps you'd like for your husband to be the leader of the home, but you're not sure if he can really do it. You can dig into God's Word for the courage you need to let go. Lynn Donovan's husband isn't a Christian and that can lead to conflict in decision making and daily life. She found her husband's unbelief pushing her to read the Bible more. She needed to really learn what it meant to love her husband through the power of Jesus Christ.

I had a lot of selfishness and a lot of expectations of this man who was merely a human being. I finally made a daily morning appointment with the King of kings to read God's Word and pray, and that changed my life. Having God's Word pour over me, I learned to let go of my selfishness. I learned to surrender some things. I pray and give Him my frustrations. I pray and ask Him to fill me up with His love. I pray and ask the Holy Spirit to come into my midst. What's so great about the living God of the universe, He filled in those gaps that my mortal, imperfect husband couldn't. [8]

Are you ready for God to fill in the gaps? Are you ready for your husband to become the man God wants him to be? It all begins with one step down so your husband can take one step up to the plate. Let him lead. You'll be glad you did.

Today's Picture

Imagine yourself standing on a stage that represents your home. You are holding a microphone, calling out directions. Your husband is seated in the front row, waiting for you to hand over the microphone to him because he has something to say. Do you hand the microphone to him cheerfully or grudgingly?

Today's Prayer

Lord, be glorified in my home. Help me to trust my husband's leadership as we work together as a team. Show me how to encourage him as a man and a leader. I humble myself before You and ask You to bring Your order and peace to my marriage.

Proud to Serve

"The LORD gave and the LORD has taken away;
may the name of the LORD be praised."

JOB 1:21

What if you have yielded to God and your husband, yet trouble has compounded in your life? How can you find joy in the midst of unbearable circumstances? Every wife goes through seasons of pain and trial. Maybe it's marital trouble or financial crisis. Or, as in the case of Carol Kent, it's a child in desperate need.

Carol and her husband, Gene, had been happily married for many years. They were proud of their only child, Jason, who was a graduate of the US Naval Academy and heading into a great career. But as quickly as you could flip a light switch, the Kents' lives went from sunny to black. Their son Jason had been charged with first-degree murder.

Jason had married a previously married woman with two little girls, and there were multiple allegations of abuse from their biological father. It looked like that father was about to get unsupervised visitation with the girls, and Jason began to unravel. He became fixated on eliminating that threat of abuse and harm to his family. He disastrously took the role of avenger and shot his wife's ex-husband. Carol and Gene were thrust into a two-and-half-year wait through seven trial postponements. It was overwhelming. Carol says,

> When you face a trial of gigantic magnitude, the little things
> become big things. Gene and I found that sometimes we would
> be nitpicking at each other over little tiny things. It was crazy.

Maybe I didn't have the shelf in my bathroom all cleared up, and he would say, "This looks like a mess." And I would yell back, "Every other room in this house is ready for company right now, can't I have this one simple little space to myself?" I would start to cry, which seems so melodramatic in retrospect, but then we said, "This isn't the real issue, is it?"

We both realized we had to make a choice. We could instantly recognize that everything that went wrong seemed to be exaggerated, and it was really the big thing in our life that we had to come together for or else we wouldn't make it. I think many times people just start fighting, and then they think, *We can't make it. Our marriage is falling apart.* And often when you have a gigantic crisis in a family, you will see a marriage falling apart. Because it just becomes so hard to keep communicating without emotion coming into it.

A Difficult Verdict

In 2002, Jason was found guilty of murder in the first degree. He was sentenced to a lifetime in prison. Through his letters from prison, he's participated in every chapter of Carol's book *Between a Rock and a Grace Place.* He is genuinely remorseful, and his parents miss him greatly. Carol shares,

> I'll walk by a closet and see a naval academy uniform, and I will just have that overwhelming sense that that life will never be ours again. And so we give each other permission to grieve. Even though we have a joy and a happiness in our hearts that can only be explained in the supernatural dimension, it is okay to give ourselves permission to have some grieving days as well. Because otherwise it just becomes a Pollyanna plastic smile that we slap on and say, "Hey, God is good. Heaven is tomorrow and everything is going to be okay." We sometimes forget we live in a very fallen world where bad things happen even to Christian people.
>
> Joy is a process. You begin by communicating daily with God. Sometimes that splash of joy comes in a Scripture verse that leaps off the page when you read it. We don't have the life we wanted, but we do have a life that is filled with purpose and even joy because of what God has allowed us to do with this horrible thing that has happened. So we had a choice to use it as a

platform on which we can give hope to others, and that brings us a lot of joy.

Another way to keep the joy and find the happiness is to be sure to stay involved with people. Because when you go through a difficult place, it's natural to cocoon and to not be available. That really is the time when you most need to be with at least one other person.

Do yourself a favor and take this advice from a godly woman who has endured more than most of us will ever experience. *Allow yourself to grieve. Communicate with God daily. Keep looking for His splashes of joy. Use your hardships as a platform to give hope to others. Stay involved with people.*

Divine Multiplication

I saw a pickup truck with large words printed on the back window: "Happy to be here, proud to serve." That sounds like a fitting attitude for someone who is serving Christ, doesn't it? We are happy to be part of God's family and we're proud to serve Him wherever He may send us. Maybe you've been through hard times and found yourself at odds with your husband simply because you're at odds with life. Remember, there is joy waiting for you when you yield to your husband and value him above yourself, even when you are hurting. Listen to these words from Carol:

> The real answer to finding the joy of yielding is that there is something almost supernatural and very godly that happens when we yield to our husband and when we yield to God. You find the joy that you bring to that person is so great that they just pour love all over you in return. It's about partnering with each other. One yields to one, the other yields back. It's like when you fall into the embrace of God. You feel Him loving you and you just can't resist it. And then you want to love Him even more. It's a multiplication type of thing.[9]

My eight-year-old son, Ethan, has what's called Minuto Loco (the Crazy Minute) in math class every day. It's a drill of how many multiplication problems students can complete in one minute. The goal is ninety. That's crazy, right? You may think it's crazy to yield to your husband and to God during times of crisis. But remember, it's a little like crazy math.

When you yield to your husband, he'll more easily yield toward you, and the happiness in your home will multiply.

Don't let the hard times divide you from your spouse. Attack the problem, not each other. Lean into the strong arms of God and get ready to watch Him work with splashes of joy and divine multiplication.

Today's Picture

If you are experiencing a major disappointment in your life, use the following as a to-do list and picture yourself checking off each one:

- ❑ Allow yourself to grieve.

- ❑ Communicate with God daily.

- ❑ Keep looking for His splashes of joy.

- ❑ Use your hardships as a platform to give hope to others.

- ❑ Stay involved with people, especially your husband.

Today's Prayer

Lord, You can do anything! You can make a way in the wilderness and streams in the desert. Come and do a new thing in my life. Renew my hope and joy right now as I pray. I yield myself completely to Your plan and will for my life. I will look for Your splashes of joy today. I will not allow Satan to divide me from my husband. Instead we run under the shadow of the Almighty and ask that You deliver us from evil.

Day 30

Going Bananas

But the fruit of the Spirit is love, joy, peace, forbearance,
kindness, goodness, faithfulness, gentleness and self-control.

GALATIANS 5:22-23

What kind of fruit is your marriage yielding? When Hayley DiMarco got married, her first year of marriage wasn't yielding much sweet fruit. Instead, it was yielding a lot of broken plates. She and her husband, Michael, were in their thirties and set in their ways when they married. The courtship was dreamy, but when it was time to combine lives and households, their worlds turned upside down. In her book *The Fruitful Wife*, Hayley writes:

> We didn't understand anything about each other except that we didn't understand each other. Our fights seemed monumental. And so was our frustration and anger. In order to save our bedroom door and fine china, we both took action. Michael bought a punching bag, and I went to Goodwill and bought an armful of cheap plates. Our basement/garage was subterranean and covered with a thick rock wall. So we set up our "anger management" stations in the garage with a big pile of ceramic plates for me and a punching bag for him. Every time that we argued, which was almost every day, I would run downstairs and pick up a plate and scream as I sent it careening into the wall.

> Before marriage, the fruitful life came easily...But after marriage the fruitful life stood in direct opposition to my feelings of bitterness, anger, doubt, and pain. And I came to realize that the fruit of the Spirit doesn't show itself so much when life is a dream,

when there is no chaffing, no trials, no suffering, and no compromise. What shows itself in those moments of perfection is the fruit of the flesh seen in Romans 8:5: "For those who live according to the flesh set their minds on the things of the flesh." [10]

The flesh acts well when everything is going well. But it's only by the Holy Spirit that we can continue to bear sweet fruit—even when we'd rather throw a plate!

Banana Peel Races

Speaking of fruit, one especially memorable birthday party for James included our first—and last—banana peel race. My husband, who's a Realtor, had taken our living room furniture to stage a vacant home he was selling. Since we had an empty room, we decided to take advantage of the space to do something zany at his party. Picture a relay race with one person sitting in a chair and another person pushing that chair around a cone and back. Put a banana peel under each leg of the chair, and you've got a speed cart!

The kids and the adults loved racing around our living room, skating along on banana peels. It left a slippery mess behind, so naturally the losing team got to mop the wood floor afterward (thanks guys!). Just like that banana peel underneath the chair gave it speed and power, the Holy Spirit can empower you to do things in your marriage that you can't do alone.

You are not expected to be able to be consistently loving, joyful, peaceful, patient, kind, good, faithful, gentle, and self-controlled on your own. But you can be these desirable qualities when you yield yourself to God's Holy Spirit and allow Him to grow that fruit in you.

As a wife, maybe you've sat down for that banana peel race, ready to glide and to be led by God's Holy Spirit. But then you get pushed somewhere you don't want to go, and you want off the ride. Dena Fuller remembers when her life's fruit didn't match up with her expectations.

Who doesn't wish they were a missionary who could count the souls and orphans saved? There are times when I berate myself, *Why aren't you doing X, Y, or Z?* Then God reels me back in. "It's not what you're doing, Dena. It's who you are. You are Mine, and I am calling you to Me." The doing flows out of the relationship. It's abiding in Christ. He's the vine and I'm the branch. The fruit

that is borne is not mine to choose. I don't get to decide whether
I bear apples or grapes or bananas. That's not mine to choose. I
just have to abide in Him. [11]

Perhaps the fruit you are bearing right now in your marriage isn't
exactly what you had pictured. But as long as you are abiding in Christ
and living in accordance with His Word, take heart and hold on.

Insanity

You've probably heard the quote that insanity is doing the same thing
over and over again and expecting different results. Case in point: I was
trying to upload three photos of my kids onto my Facebook page. After a
long time, the second and third picture showed up, but not the first. Frus-
trated, I did the exact same process again with the same result. After failing a third time, I realized I'd better try something different. I waited until
the first picture appeared before attempting to upload the second photo.
That did the trick!

When the fruit of the Spirit you want to bear in your marriage isn't
quite "uploading," it's a good time to step back and ask yourself if there's
something you could be doing differently. You may continue to get the
same dissatisfactory results if you don't make a change. Do you respond to
your husband in the flesh or in the Spirit? In other words, do you go with
your gut reaction or do you ask God to give you wisdom before you speak?

Being pruned isn't a fun process, but it yields fruit if you allow yourself to be corrected and to learn from your mistakes. As it says in Hebrews
12:11, "No discipline seems pleasant at the time, but painful. Later on,
however, it produces a harvest of righteousness and peace for those who
have been trained by it."

Sweet Fruit

Thankfully for Hayley DiMarco those days of breaking plates are long
gone. She and Michael are enjoying the sweet fruit of the Holy Spirit in
their marriage and teaching others to do the same. Hayley writes about
the war that wages within the heart of every wife:

> This battle between the flesh and the Spirit isn't spoken of as
> much as the symptoms of the battle are spoken of. Our feelings
> of betrayal, of hurt, of rejection, of abandonment, of isolation,

and of frustration are often talked about, but they are not the cause or the root of the problem—only the symptoms. The root lies in our spiritual barrenness, our lack of the fruit of the Spirit. [12]

Like Hayley, we as wives must hunger for God to fill us with the fruit of the Spirit. In order for love, joy, peace, and kindness to grow, the soil of our hearts must be soft and ready to yield. No more barren days, doing this wife thing in our own strength and abilities. Instead, it's time to rely on God's power and submit to His Spirit in our marriages. The result will be a harvest of sweet, overflowing fruit—more fruit than you can even imagine!

Today's Picture

You are staring at a delicious fruit basket. Your mouth begins to water as you look at the colorful apples, oranges, bananas, strawberries, blueberries, and kiwis. None of the fruit is rotten. In fact, much of the fruit looks supersized.

Today's Prayer

Lord, I want my marriage to bear sweet fruit like that fruit basket. I don't want anything rotten in my marriage—no unforgiveness, bitterness, malice, pride, or envy. I turn my back on those things. Fill me with the Holy Spirit and help me to bear fruit that is pleasing to You. May the fruit of the Spirit—love, joy, peace, forbearance, kindness, goodness, faithfulness, gentleness, and self-control—be evident in my life today.

Day 31

A Lasting Joy

Live in harmony with one another.

ROMANS 12:16

One of my favorite sounds is James playing the piano. While we were dating, if we passed a piano in a department store or lobby, James would sit on the bench and begin to play. He's a free spirit, so he figured the worst thing that could happen is someone would tell him to stop. I can't remember anyone ever asking him to stop. His beautiful melodies always improved any room.

Before we had James's gorgeous childhood piano in our home, we had a freebie piano. Playing this piano was like driving a Ford Pinto, but we couldn't complain. We got it free from our neighbor when he moved. Since the piano wasn't worth much, James decided to tune it himself after watching several YouTube videos on the subject. He asked for my help, and that's when the trouble began.

"Don't touch the hammers!" he said emphatically.

I didn't even know what a hammer was. He wanted me to lie under the piano and line up two points at the bottom while he held something at the top. I tried my best, but I couldn't quite see how to line them up properly. My head hurt from lying on the pedals.

"I need a pillow!" I said, which James thought was a ridiculous request.

"Get yourself where you can see it!" he said. "Line up the point in the back first!"

I wondered which one was the back. I couldn't see a thing, and I didn't understand what he wanted me to do. He was getting tenser and I was getting more defensive. After many unsuccessful attempts, he said to forget it. He would figure it out himself. I was relieved of my piano duty, which was a relief, but I remember feeling totally lame.

"I need your help!" he barked a few minutes later.

"But you told me to go away!"

I tried again to line it all up and still couldn't do it. Finally, he got it to snap together all by himself.

This piano-tuning experience had been the low point of our day. Nothing harmonious about it. I told him I wasn't wired to do stuff like that and that I truly couldn't figure it out. He was baffled that I couldn't do something that seemed so simple to him.

When trying to achieve that beautiful note of harmony and unity in a marriage, sometimes everything doesn't line up quite right.

The Note of Unity

When you and your husband said "I do," the Bible tells us that you both became one. What a mystery of losing yourself and finding yourself all at the same time. The happiest of marriages strive to keep that note of unity, working as a team, yielding to each other willingly for a lifetime. Marjorie Blanchard says,

> One of the things Ken and I strive for is to be unified in the decisions we make, particularly the big decisions like moving or a big purchase or quitting a job. If God wanted us both to think exactly alike, we wouldn't even be a couple. When Ken and I work hard to achieve a unified point of view, then our decisions are usually better. If we can't come to unity, we generally postpone making the decision. We collect more information so we can be in a better position to be unified in our decisions. [13]

God's best plan for marriage is for a husband and wife to experience unity. Genesis 2:24 says they were created to become "one flesh." But sin in the Garden of Eden so long ago introduced:

Blame—"She made me eat that fruit!"

Shame—"I was afraid because I was naked; so I hid."

Pain—The drama unfolds with childbirth and the struggle for control.

It takes hard work to achieve unity in marriage. In the New Testament, some Pharisees tested Jesus by asking Him if it was lawful for a man to divorce his wife. Jesus asked what Moses had commanded.

They said, "Moses permitted a man to write a certificate of divorce and send her away."

"It was because your hearts were hard that Moses wrote you this law," Jesus replied. "But at the beginning of creation God 'made them male and female.' For this reason a man will leave his father and mother and be united to his wife, and the two will become one flesh. So they are no longer two, but one flesh. Therefore what God has joined together, let no one separate" (Mark 10:4-9).

I want you to pause and consider Jesus's pointed words: *It was because your hearts were hard.* We must diligently guard our hearts from becoming hardened like that. One way to keep your heart soft and pliable before God and your husband is to be constantly teachable. Proverbs 29:18 (HCSB) says, "One who listens to instruction will be happy."

Happiness is often portrayed as doing things your way. But lasting happiness is truly found in doing things God's way.

Give Massages (Even When You Don't Feel Like It)

It was that time of the month, and I wasn't feeling one ounce of tenderness for James. He had done nothing wrong; I was just plain irritable. Since I write about being a happy wife, I thought I'd do an experiment on myself. I would act lovey-dovey and sweet toward James and see if my feelings would follow.

I proclaimed to James with much fanfare at the end of a long day, "I will give you a ten-minute massage!" Did I *feel* like giving him a ten-minute massage? No way. I wanted to *receive* a ten-minute massage! And do you know what? After that simple ten minutes of serving my spouse, I felt so much more relaxed.

God has wired it so that we receive the blessing when we set out to bless someone else. I was the one who served, yet I felt happier and refreshed. It takes a measure of faith to act in a loving way when we don't feel like it. But when we step out in faith, the by-product more often than not is happiness.

Although your 31-day experiment in happiness at home is coming to a close, your journey of fresh joy is certainly under way. After all sorts of soul searching and experimentation, King Solomon wrote in Ecclesiastes 3:12, "I know that there is nothing better for people than to be happy and to do good while they live."

While you do good works in your marriage, striving to hit that note of unity with your husband, you will experience a smile that will not expire. You'll have a lasting joy to carry you through the years to come. "Happily ever after" isn't only for fairy-tale princesses. It's for you. But "happily ever after" won't look like a couple on a horse riding off into the sunset. It will be real.

Today's Picture

The sign "Happily Ever After" hangs above a prominent door in your house. These are not just sentimental words. You are utterly, immovably convinced that all your days with your husband will be blessed and happy.

Today's Prayer

Lord, I thank You for this 31-day journey of becoming a happy wife. With my whole heart, I desire to have unity with my husband. Make us one. Help me to serve him—even when I don't feel like it. May I experience the lasting joy of having a marriage that pleases and glorifies You. I know You want my husband and me to live happily ever after. Draw us closer to You and to each other every day. We want our marriage to shine as a bright light for You.

Conclusion

So Happiness Isn't a Feeling?

I n the past 31 days, you've noticed that happiness isn't defined as that feeling you get when your husband comes home with dinner and roses. Happiness is more like a gift you receive when you choose to be grateful. Remember what life was like before you met your husband? You longed for someone tall, dark, and handsome to sweep you away from a life of loneliness. I love this little story from Charlie Jones:

> The professor of English was trying to drum into his class the importance of a large vocabulary. "I assure you," he said, "if you repeat a word ten or twelve times, it will be yours forever." In the back of the room a cute coed took a deep breath, closed her eyes and whispered, "Richard, Richard, Richard..."[1]

Many days ago, you whispered your husband's name over and over again, and you got what you wanted! When James and I were engaged, he lived in Dallas and I lived in Virginia Beach. We wrote letters almost daily. Here's something I wrote to him on July 10, 1998:

> Dear Cute Boy,
>
> I can't wait to see you! I am counting the days. It'll be so wonderful to see your face and hold your hand and smell your neck and kiss your lips—a little bit of heaven right here on earth.

I'm giggling now as I read those words. I was giddy with love back then. Today, when James comes home from work, I will see his face. I can hold his hand and smell his neck and kiss his lips. But will I think, *Ah, heaven on earth?* When I make a point to remember where we've come from, it makes a big difference, doesn't it? You must take the time to remember your past with gratitude. You don't sit idly by, waiting for that feeling of happiness to overtake you, waiting for your husband to wow you once more. You act first by thinking differently—by thinking *gratefully.* Then that wonderful feeling of happiness will rush in behind those positive thoughts of thanksgiving.

When Unhappy Days Come

No doubt your husband will say something insensitive to you and hurt your feelings—maybe even before you fall asleep tonight. Unhappy moments in a marriage are bound to come. The question is how are you going to respond? You must believe that it's not your husband's job to make you happy. You are not dependent on him. It's not up to life to make you happy. You are not dependent on perfect circumstances. You must take responsibility for your own life and happiness.

Leslie Vernick gives this advice to help you manage negative emotions:

> Often people overidentify with their emotions. They'll say, "I'm so mad" or "I'm so unhappy." When they say it that way, it makes the emotion stronger than it should be because they are not their feelings. They are not their anger. They are just feeling anger. We need to teach ourselves to say, "I am aware that I'm feeling anger now." Once we have that awareness that is separate from our anger, we can do something about the anger. We now have our feelings versus our feelings having us. That makes a huge difference in how we decide to respond to the emotion we're feeling. [2]

Don't ever think of yourself or refer to yourself as an unhappy wife. Be aware of those times when you are feeling unhappiness and realize that you have control over that emotion. Unhappiness doesn't have control over you anymore.

When unhappiness knocks at the door of your heart, I want you to remember this little story about my son Ethan. He was being silly in the bathtub, pretending to be a deep-sea diver and going under the water to make his sisters laugh. One time he dunked under, and I heard this "Boom!" I cringed because I knew he had hit the bottom of the tub with his head. But instead of crying, he came up laughing. He felt embarrassed and goofy. Laughter had effectively served as anesthesia, lessoning the pain of the bonk to his head.

So the next time unhappiness knocks, greet it with a big smile and a sense of humor. If you can keep a light heart, laughing at the ups and downs of married life, your journey will have many more happy days than sad ones. Remember, a merry heart is like medicine!

Your Word of the Day

James had a life-changing encounter with Jesus in junior high. He became an outspoken Christian, carrying his Bible to school and even to parties. His nickname was Moses. He would have the "Word of the Day," a Bible verse he would write on a piece of paper and pass around class. Kids would come up to him and ask, "Hey James, what's the Word of the Day?" Decades later, I attended his class reunion, and his classmates were still asking him for the Word of the Day.

We've been focusing on five key words in this 31-day experiment of becoming a happier wife. Which of these words have resonated with you the most?

H = Becoming *Hopeful*

A = Becoming *Adaptable*

P = Becoming *Positive*

P = Becoming *Purposeful*

Y = Becoming *Yielded*

When I feel grumpy (yes, I do feel grumpy), I like to go through this checklist in my mind:

❑ Is my hope in God?

❑ Am I being adaptable and pliable?

❑ Do I have a positive attitude?

❑ Do I have a clear purpose?

❑ Am I yielded to God and to my husband?

184   31 DAYS TO BECOMING A HAPPY WIFE

Going through these five questions gives me clarity and perspective. It puts my feelings in the proper place. It helps me identify what I'm doing right, which boosts my spirits, and also helps me identify where I can make positive changes. Keep these five keys of being HAPPY in your mind and make a commitment to grow in these areas long after you turn the last page of this book.

Enjoy the Party

When my daughter Noelle turned six, we invited a few of her friends to our home for a fancy tea party. My parents were going to help serve, so I told them and James to wear a white shirt and black pants. About thirty minutes before the party, James was still wearing a T-shirt and jeans. I didn't want to nag, but I couldn't resist asking, "You're not going to wear *that* are you?"

Several minutes later, I hardly recognized him. He was wearing a white tuxedo shirt and black bow tie from his days as a waiter at a country club—during high school! Not only had he found the shirt and tie, he could still wear them. He waited on those girls as though they were royalty. One of the girls said he looked like a groom. And I couldn't have agreed more!

That day, James's thoughtfulness wowed me big time. It was a tuxedo red-letter day that I will always remember. Not every day of marriage is a tuxedo day. Actually most are jeans and T-shirt days. But that's okay. Marriage is a continual feast if you can enjoy each day you're given with the one you love.

So for now, my friend, I leave you with this Word of the Day from 1 Thessalonians 5:16-18: "Rejoice always, pray continually, give thanks in all circumstances; for this is God's will for you in Christ Jesus."

Notes

Introduction: Do You Wish You Were Happier?

1. P.L. Tan, *Encyclopedia of 7700 Illustrations: Signs of the Times* (Garland, TX: Bible Communications, Inc., 1996).

2. Dale Carnegie, *How to Win Friends and Influence People* (New York: Simon and Schuster, 1981), 71.

Focus 1: Becoming Hopeful

1. John Maxwell, *Make Today Count: The Secret of Your Success Is Determined by Your Daily Agenda* (New York: Hachette Book Group USA, 2004), 2-3.

2. Personal interview with Cindi McMenamin, February 26, 2013.

3. Susan Meissner, *The Girl in the Glass* (Colorado Springs, CO: WaterBrook Press, 2012), back cover.

4. Personal interview with Sharon Jaynes, February 25, 2013.

5. Personal interview with Amy Youssi, June 2, 2006.

6. Interview with Sharon Jaynes.

7. www.brainyquote.com/quotes/authors/z/zig_ziglar_2.html (accessed May 22, 2013).

8. Personal interview with Poppy Smith, February 18, 2013.

9. Interview with Sharon Jaynes.

10. David Hinckley, "Americans Spend 34 Hours a Week Watching TV, According to Nielsen Numbers," *New York Daily News*, September 19, 2012, www.nydailynews.com/entertainment/tv-mov ies/americans-spend-34-hours-week-watching-tv-nielsen-numbers-article-1.1162285 (accessed March 29, 2013).

11. Zig Ziglar, "Defining Success," *Success*, www.success.com/articles/1166——zig-ziglar-defining-success (accessed May 22, 2013).

12. Personal interview with Kevin Sorbo, June 24, 2011.

13. Personal interview with Leslie Vernick, March 1, 2013.

14. Cindi and Hugh McMenamin, "Give Your Spouse a Closer Connection for Valentine's Day," *Crosswalk.com*, February 6, 2013, www.crosswalk.com/family/marriage/engagement-newly weds/give-your-spouse-a-closer-connection-for-valentine-s-day.html (accessed April 2, 2013).

15. Justin D'Arms, "Envy," *The Stanford Encyclopedia of Philosophy* (Spring 2009 edition), ed. Edward N. Zalta, http://plato.stanford.edu/archives/spr2009/entries/envy/ (accessed April 2, 2013).

16. Personal interview with Lynn Donovan, February 25, 2013.

Focus 2: Becoming Adaptable

1. Interview with Leslie Vernick.

2. Personal interview with Liz Curtis Higgs, March 12, 2013.

3. Personal interview with Pam Farrel, March 5, 2013.

4. Matthew Henry, *Matthew Henry's Commentary on the Whole Bible: Complete and Unabridged in One Volume* (Peabody, MA: Hendrickson Publishers, 1994), Php 4:10-19.

5. Personal interview with Bethany Palmer, February 20, 2013.

6. Bill Hybels, Stuart Briscoe, Haddon Robinson, *Mastering Contemporary Preaching* (Portland, OR: Multnomah Press, 1989), 108-9.

7. Interview with Liz Curtis Higgs.

8. Personal interview with Carol Kent, February 26, 2013.

9. Personal interview with Marjorie Blanchard, May 8, 2013.

10. Interview with Liz Curtis Higgs.

11. Interview with Pam Farrel.

12. Personal interview with Joyce Penner, July 28, 2011.

13. Personal interview with Kathi Lipp, February 28, 2013.

14. Interview with Pam Farrel.

15. Matthew Rosenbaum, "Women and Stress: Could Your Hectic Life Be Killing You?," *ABC News*, March 6, 2012, http://abcnews.go.com/blogs/health/2012/03/06/women-and-stress-could-your-hectic-life-be-killing-you/ (accessed May 31, 2013).

16. Richard Swenson, *Margin: Restoring Emotional, Physical, Financial, and Time Reserves to Over-loaded Lives* (Colorado Springs, CO: NavPress, 1992), 13-14.

17. www.goodreads.com/author/quotes/50316.Zig_Ziglar (accessed May 30, 2013).

18. Leeana Tankersley, "Channeling Your Inner Navy SEAL, #2," *Gypsy Ink* (blog), March 26, 2013, www.gypsyink.com/2013/03/channeling-your-inner-navy-seal-2/ (accessed April 11, 2013).

Focus 3: Becoming Positive

1. Personal interview with Fawn Weaver, February 26, 2013.

2. Gary Chapman, *The One Year Love Language Minute Devotional* (Carol Stream, IL: Tyndale House Publishers, 2009), June 6.

3. Interview with Poppy Smith.

4. Interview with Kathi Lipp.

5. Sharon Jaynes, "The Danger of Ingratitude," *Sharon Jaynes* (blog), January 21, 2013, http://sharonjaynes.com/the-danger-of-ingratitude/ (accessed May 29, 2013).

6. www.goodreads.com/author/quotes/50316.Zig_Ziglar (accessed May 6, 2013).

7. Interview with Liz Curtis Higgs.

8. Sumathi Reddy, "Stress-Busting Smiles," *Wall Street Journal*, February 25, 2013, http://online.wsj.com/article/SB10001424127887323699704578326363601444362.html (accessed April 15, 2013).

9. Dale Carnegie, *How to Win Friends and Influence People* (New York: Simon and Schuster, 1981), 69.

10. Interview with Liz Curtis Higgs.

11. Personal interview with Dena Fuller, March 7, 2013.

12. Carnegie, *How to Win Friends*, 73.

13. For information about this fast, go to www.daniel-fast.com.

14. Charlie Jones, *Humor Is Tremendous* (Wheaton, IL: Tyndale House Publishers, 1988), 83.

15. Interview with Leslie Vernick.

16. Interview with Pam Farrel.

17. Interview with Marjorie Blanchard.

18. Jones, *Humor Is Tremendous*, 36.

19. Interview with Sharon Jaynes.

Focus 4: Becoming Purposeful

1. Matthew Henry, *Matthew Henry's Commentary on the Whole Bible: Complete and Unabridged in One Volume* (Peabody, MA: Hendrickson Publishers, 1994), Prov. 31:10-31.

2. Interview with Bethany Palmer.

3. Interview with Leslie Vernick.

4. Clifford and Joyce Penner, *The Gift of Sex: A Guide to Sexual Fulfillment* (Nashville, TN: Thomas Nelson, 2003), 197.

5. Bill and Pam Farrel, *Red-Hot Monogamy: Making Your Marriage Sizzle* (Eugene, OR: Harvest House Publishers, 2006), 111.

6. Interview with Pam Farrel.

7. Interview with Liz Curtis Higgs.

8. Interview with Kathi Lipp.

9. Interview with Cindi McMenamin.

10. Charlie Jones, *Humor Is Tremendous* (Wheaton, IL: Tyndale House Publishers, 1988), 37.

11. Interview with Sharon Jaynes.

12. "Modern Marriage," *Pew Research Center*, July 18, 2007, www.pewsocialtrends.org/2007/07/18/modern-marriage/ (accessed April 28, 2013).

13. Peggy Noonan, *When Character Was King: A Story of Ronald Reagan* (New York: Penguin Group, 2001), 187.

14. P.L. Tan, *Encyclopedia of 7700 Illustrations: Signs of the Times* (Garland, TX: Bible Communications, 1996).

15. Interview with Pam Farrel.

16. Interview with Carol Kent.

17. *oChristian.com*, "Christian Quotes," http://christian-quotes.ochristian.com/christian-quotes_ochristian.cgi?query=bored&action=Search&x=0&y=0 (accessed April 29, 2013).

18. Interview with Marjorie Blanchard.

19. Interview with Sharon Jaynes.

20. Interview with Marjorie Blanchard.

21. Interview with Kathi Lipp.

22. Interview with Dena Fuller.

23. Stormie Omartian, *The Power of a Praying Wife* (Eugene, OR: Harvest House Publishers, 1997), 18.

Focus 5: Becoming Yielded

1. Karen Ehman, *Let. It. Go.: How to Stop Running the Show and Start Walking in Faith* (Grand Rapids, MI: Zondervan, 2012), 68.

2. Denny Davis, "Marriage Humor," www.dennydavis.net/poemfiles/mrg2.htm (accessed May 2, 2013).

3. Interview with Liz Curtis Higgs.

4. Interview with Cindi McMenamin.

5. Chris Montgomery, "The Queen of Worry," *An Everyday Voice* (blog), March 28, 2013, www.aneverydayvoice.com/2013/03/the-queen-of-worry.html (accessed May 7, 2013).

6. John Wooden and Steve Jamison, *Wooden: A Lifetime of Observations and Reflections On and Off the Court* (Chicago: Contemporary Books, 1997), 19.

7. Dennis Rainey, *Stepping Up: A Call to Courageous Manhood* (Little Rock, AR: Family Life Publishing, 2011), 5.

8. Interview with Lynn Donovan.

9. Interview with Carol Kent.

10. Hayley DiMarco, *The Fruitful Wife* (Wheaton, IL: Crossway, 2012), 10.

11. Interview with Dena Fuller.

12. DiMarco, *The Fruitful Wife*, 12.

13. Interview with Marjorie Blanchard.

Conclusion: So Happiness Isn't a Feeling?

1. Charlie Jones, *Humor Is Tremendous* (Wheaton, IL: Tyndale House Publishers, 1988), 106.

2. Interview with Leslie Vernick.

Daily Affirmations of the Happy Wife

- I, _____, am a happy wife who lives with integrity and gratitude. I am a peacemaker, and I look for the good in every situation. I believe my marriage is my most valuable human relationship, and I will celebrate life with my spouse every day.

- I am filled with *hope* for the future. I place my trust in God alone and know that my marriage is safe in His hands.

- I am *adaptable*, not set in my ways. I am willing to learn and change when it's necessary and beneficial.

- I am a *positive* and uplifting wife. I choose to smile frequently, forgive easily, and build my husband up daily with my words.

- I am a woman of *purpose*. I set goals for my marriage and reach them. I am prayerful, disciplined, consistent, and on fire with passion for my marriage. I believe my marriage will impact generations to come.

- I am *yielded* to God and to my husband. My heart is soft, I am ready to listen. I am humble, not proud. I do not complain. I choose to give thanks.

- I fully intend to live with joy and develop my marriage to bring honor and glory to God.

Bible Verses About Happiness

But let all who take refuge in you be glad;
    let them ever sing for joy.
Spread your protection over them,
    that those who love your name may rejoice in you.
Surely, Lord, you bless the righteous;
    you surround them with your favor as with a shield.
(Psalm 5:11-12)

Happy is the nation whose God is Yahweh—
the people He has chosen to be His own possession!
(Psalm 33:12 HCSB)

Taste and see that the Lord is good.
How happy is the man who takes refuge in Him!
(Psalm 34:8 HCSB)

How happy is the man
who has put his trust in the Lord
and has not turned to the proud
or to those who run after lies!
(Psalm 40:4 HCSB)

See how happy the man is God corrects;
so do not reject the discipline of the Almighty.
(Job 5:17 HCSB)

How happy is the one You choose
and bring near to live in Your courts!
We will be satisfied with the goodness of Your house,
the holiness of Your temple.

(Psalm 65:4 HCSB)

But may the righteous be glad
    and rejoice before God;
    may they be happy and joyful.
Sing to God, sing in praise of his name,
    extol him who rides on the clouds;
    rejoice before him—his name is the LORD.

(Psalm 68:3-4)

How happy are those who reside in Your house,
who praise You continually.
Happy are the people whose strength is in You,
whose hearts are set on pilgrimage...
Happy is the person who trusts in You,
LORD of hosts!

(Psalm 84:4-5,12 HCSB)

Blessed are those who have learned to acclaim you,
    who walk in the light of your presence, LORD.
They rejoice in your name all day long;
    they celebrate your righteousness.

(Psalm 89:15-16)

LORD, happy is the man You discipline
and teach from Your law.

(Psalm 94:12 HCSB)

How happy are those who uphold justice,
who practice righteousness at all times.

(Psalm 106:3 HCSB)

Hallelujah!
Happy is the man who fears the LORD,
taking great delight in His commands.

(Psalm 112:1 HCSB)

How happy are those whose way is blameless,
who live according to the LORD's instruction!

(Psalm 119:1 HCSB)

How happy is everyone who fears the LORD,
who walks in His ways!
You will surely eat
what your hands have worked for.
You will be happy,
and it will go well for you.

(Psalm 128:1-2 HCSB)

Happy is the man who finds wisdom
and who acquires understanding...
[Wisdom] is a tree of life to those who embrace her,
and those who hold on to her are happy.

(Proverbs 3:13,18 HCSB)

A happy heart makes the face cheerful,
    but heartache crushes the spirit...
All the days of the oppressed are wretched,
    but the cheerful heart has a continual feast.

(Proverbs 15:13,15)

The one who understands a matter finds success,
and the one who trusts in the LORD will be happy.

(Proverbs 16:20 HCSB)

The one who lives with integrity is righteous;
his children who come after him will be happy.

(Proverbs 20:7 HCSB)

Happy is the one who is always reverent,
but one who hardens his heart falls into trouble.
                                    (Proverbs 28:14 HCSB)

Without revelation people run wild,
but one who listens to instruction will be happy.
                                    (Proverbs 29:18 HCSB)

To the person who pleases him, God gives wisdom, knowledge
and happiness (Ecclesiastes 2:26).

I know that there is nothing better for people than to be happy
and to do good while they live (Ecclesiastes 3:12).

Therefore the LORD is waiting to show you mercy,
and is rising up to show you compassion,
for the LORD is a just God.
All who wait patiently for Him are happy.
                                    (Isaiah 30:18 HCSB)

"His master replied, 'Well done, good and faithful servant! You
have been faithful with a few things; I will put you in charge of
many things. Come and share your master's happiness!'" (Matthew 25:21).

Though you have not seen him, you love him; and even though
you do not see him now, you believe in him and are filled with an
inexpressible and glorious joy, for you are receiving the end result
of your faith, the salvation of your souls (1 Peter 1:8-9).

The Happy Wives Discussion Guide

Focus 1: Becoming Hopeful

When you think of your marriage, are you filled more with hope or doubt?

Tell the story of how you met your husband.

Whose responsibility is it to make you happy: yours or your husband's? Why?

How can you fight the tendency to take your husband for granted?

Instead of completing the sentence "I would be happy if…," complete this sentence: "I am happy because…"

Have you experienced a new dose of hope when you pray or when you praise God?

What are some practical things you can do this week to lessen your screen time (phones, TV, movies, social media) and increase your spouse time?

Focus 2: Becoming Adaptable

Describe a time in your marriage when you didn't want to do something your husband wanted. Did you reach a compromise? Stage a protest? Do it his way? What happened?

When life throws you and your husband a curveball, are you able to adapt and make changes easily?

Would you characterize yourself more like flint (hard and set in your ways) or like clay (soft and easily moldable)?

When you are disappointed in something your husband has done, how do you normally respond? Ideally, how would you like to respond?

Philippians 4:12 says, "I have learned the secret of being content in any and every situation, whether well fed or hungry, whether living in plenty or in want." Where are you in this process of learning contentment?

Do you have plenty of energy or are you tired most days? Do you get a good night's sleep? What is one change you can make in order to get more rest?

How much of the conflict in your marriage centers on finances? What's one thing you can do to become more financially responsible and resourceful?

Remember Kathi Lipp's salad kit (the lotions and oils to spice up their love life)? Do you have your own version of the salad kit? (I give you permission to skip this if you are blushing!) What are practical ways you can adapt your weekly schedule to make more time for intimacy with your husband?

Focus 3: Becoming Positive

Do you consider yourself more of a "glass half empty" or a "glass half full" kind of girl?

Share three things you appreciate about your spouse (you can share more if there's time).

Do you agree that it's socially more acceptable to complain about your spouse to friends than it is to praise him?

Is it difficult for you to control the words that come out of your mouth? Do you struggle with anger or using hurtful words toward your husband?

If all the words you said to your husband in one week were recorded, what do you think the ratio would be between "put-downs" and "put-ups"?

Make it a goal to smile at your husband at least five times per day for one week. These are five separate times in the day, so smiling at him five times in five minutes doesn't count. Try a smile upon waking, one at breakfast, another one after work, one while doing dishes, and another one at bedtime. Report to the group any changes you feel or notice.

Complete this sentence: "It's easy being married to my husband because…" Now imagine that the opposite were true about your husband. Aren't you grateful for the guy you've got?

How do you keep grudges from getting in between you and your man?

Focus 4: Becoming Purposeful

Did you do the smile exercise from the last set of questions? How did smiling on purpose boost your mood?

Do you struggle with perfectionism?

Picture if being a wife were your full-time profession. What strengths and weaknesses do you bring to the job? What are a few activities or new skills that would add to your resume?

Most of the time, do you feel connected or disconnected to your husband? What are ways you can connect more often with your spouse in your current schedule?

When was your last date and what did you do? (If you can't remember, Friday night is coming!)

How do you keep your marriage from becoming boring? What are ways you stay interesting to yourself and to your husband?

How have you seen your prayers affect your husband? Affect you?

Focus 5: Becoming Yielded

Attention women who want control (that's most of us): How have you found freedom in giving control over to God?

The husband is the head of the marriage. Discuss.

How does stress increase in your marriage when you try to control your circumstances? How does stress decrease as you give your concerns over to God?

John Wooden wrote, "Don't be stubborn and insist on having your own way. Look to find a way that works for both of you." Why do you think this is an important principle for your marriage?

How have troubles in life brought you closer to God and closer to your spouse?

What evidence do you see of the fruit of the Spirit (Galatians 5:22-23) working in your marriage?

Give an example of something you did to serve your husband even when you didn't feel like it. How did you feel after doing something kind?

Wrap-Up Questions

Of all the areas of becoming a happy wife, which focus challenged you the most?

H: Becoming Hopeful
A: Becoming Adaptable
P: Becoming Positive
P: Becoming Purposeful
Y: Becoming Yielded

What changes in your attitude have occurred in the last 31 days?

As you have focused on becoming happier and acting happier, did the feelings of happiness follow?

What is something you learned about happiness while reading this book?

Has your husband noticed anything different about you?

What are a few specific things you are going to continue to do after this 31-day experiment is over?

1.

2.

3.

Visit Arlene's website for bonus material

www.ArlenePellicane.com

- Listen to Arlene's podcast for the interviews of many wives featured in this book, such as Liz Curtis Higgs, Carol Kent, and Pam Farrel.
- Enhance your reading with corresponding videos from Arlene.
- Interact with Arlene through her blog.
- Find creative date ideas to connect more often with your man.
- Sign up for Arlene's free monthly newsletter with tips for the happy home.

To learn more about Harvest House books
and to read sample chapters, visit our website:

www.harvesthousepublishers.com

HARVEST HOUSE PUBLISHERS
EUGENE, OREGON

Acknowledgments

Thank you to all the happy wives who allowed me to interview them for this book. Your insights have wowed me, and I'm forever grateful for your generous support of this happy-home project.

Dr. Marjorie Blanchard—I am so glad we met at Professional Women's Fellowship. Thank you for your kindness in sharing your personal stories and for your leadership expertise.

Lynn Donovan—You radiate the love of Christ. What an example you are to me and many others of being joyfully committed to your Savior and your spouse.

Pam Farrel—Sending up a big "whoop whoop" to my amazing mentor who has believed in me and guided me through this author life. You are priceless. Thank you for showing scores of wives through your bright example how to be happy.

Dena Fuller—I was honored to talk with you and felt immediately as if I were speaking to an old friend. I appreciate your honesty and depth. You have made your family your focus, and the world is a richer place because of it.

Liz Curtis Higgs—I so admire your speaking and writing, and to have you in my book—pinch me, I'm dreaming. What a joy! Thank you for brightening Bill's world and our world with that red-lipstick smile.

Sharon Jaynes—You are a "Girlfriend in God" to thousands, and I was touched that you took the time to be a part of my book. Thank you for showing women that it's possible to overcome your past and purposefully build a God-honoring, happy home.

Carol Kent—Getting to know you and Gene at the Faithlife Conference was a huge highlight for me. You are the quintessential author and speaker. Thank you for sharing your life's journey with others in order to bring hope.

Kathi Lipp—Mama Chick, my book is funnier, realer (is that a word?), and more meaningful because of you. I love your enthusiasm and passion to help and inspire others. I am very thankful to call you friend.

Cindi McMenamin—You have been such a dear encouragement to me. Thank you for your always kind words and readiness to support me. Thank you for lending your wisdom to the book.

Bethany Palmer—Meeting you at *The Better Show* was no coincidence. You and Scott are not only The Money Couple, you are one very happy couple! Thank you for sharing your recipe for success with my readers.

Poppy Smith—You help us all answer that question, "Why can't he be more like me?" Thank you for your candor and example of growing together—not apart—despite differences. You were a joy to talk with.

Leslie Vernick—You have an amazing gift of helping people define what is wrong in their relationships. Then you teach us how to take the next step to wholeness. Thank you for sharing practical wisdom gained from your life and practice as a Christian counselor.

Fawn Weaver—It's wonderful to know a kindred spirit who believes in living happily ever after. Love rocks! Thank you for sharing the unique and hilarious story of how you met Keith and how you became a happy wife yourself.

To my husband, James—I certainly could not be a happy wife without you! You're my main ingredient, favorite person, number one friend, and greatest love. Thank you for being my source for funny stories and for letting me actually share those stories with others. You are my happily ever after come true.

To my kids, Ethan, Noelle, and Lucy—I am way blessed to be your mom. Thanks, Ethan, for keeping me on track with my writing. Noelle, your pictures on my desk make me smile. Lucy, I am grateful for your love for trying on my shoes, which has kept you happily occupied while I write. As you grow into adults, may you always live in a happy home.

To my mother, Ann, and mother-in-love, Marilyn—Thank you for being happy wives of character, virtue, and joy.

To my Harvest House family—Thank you for believing in the message of this book. I am so blessed to work with all of you. Thanks especially to my editor, Rod Morris, and to LaRae Weikert, Christianne Debysingh, Brad Moses, and Shane White.

About Arlene Pellicane

Arlene and her happy husband, James, live in San Diego, California, with their three children, Ethan, Noelle, and Lucy. Arlene is also the author of *31 Days to a Happy Husband* and *31 Days to a Younger You*. Before becoming a stay-at-home mom, Arlene worked as the associate producer for *Turning Point Television* with Dr. David Jeremiah as well as a features producer for *The 700 Club*. She received her BA in intercultural studies from Biola University and her master's in journalism from Regent University.

Arlene has appeared as a guest on *The 700 Club*, *Turning Point with Dr. David Jeremiah*, *The Better Show*, *The Hour of Power*, *TLC's Home Made Simple*, and *Family Life Today*. An energetic communicator, she shares humorous and compelling stories to guide women to positive life change. For free resources along with information about contacting Arlene to speak at your event, visit www.ArlenePellicane.com.

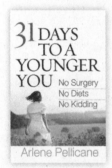